Peeling an Orange

Peeling an Orange
Practicing without being a saint

Stephen Peter Anderson

Copyright © 2024 by Stephen Peter Anderson

All rights reserved. No part of this book may be reproduced in any form or by any electronic or mechanical means, including information storage and retrieval systems, without written permission from the author, except for the use of brief quotations in a book review.

Stephen Peter Anderson has no responsibility for the persistence or accuracy of URL's for external or third-party Internet Websites referred to in this publication and does not guarantee that any content on such websites is, or will remain, accurate or appropriate.

Published in Sydney, Australia, by ZuluAlpha Press a registered trademark. www.zulualphapress.com. In some instances, names, dates, location, and other details have been changed to protect the identity and privacy of those discussed in this book.

Printed and bound in Australia.

ISBN 978-0-6484692-1-6

To my wife for always being patient with me.
To Ferne and Ivy for always reminding me to always practice patience.

Contents

Preface	xi

Part One
Essence of Patience

1. Divine Timing: Patience from Creation's Beginning	3
2. Virtues of Patience	16
3. The Spectrum of Patience: From Stillness to Action	25
4. Waiting Well	36
5. Resilient Living: Endurance and Perseverance in Practice	45
6. Losing your Patience	55

Part Two
Cultivating Patience

7. The Practice of Patience	69
8. The Beauty in Stillness	78
9. How to Peel an Orange	87
10. Wisdom in Waiting	102
11. The Formation of Character	111
12. Waiting for God	121

Part Three
Acts Of Patience

13. Harvesting the Fourth Fruit	137
14. Enduring Grace: The Interplay of Tolerance and Patience	145
15. A God Given Restraint	159
16. Patience and Love: An Unlikely Partnership	169

Conclusion	177
Acknowledgments	181
Scriptural Index	183
Glossary	187
About the Author	191
Also by Stephen Peter Anderson	193

Paper is more patient than people

— Anne Frank

Preface

Patience may seem a strange subject to discuss given the current climate at which I first started writing this. The world was engulfed in a pandemic that, for the most part, appeared to be contained at best but nowhere near its end. Lockdowns, varying in severity depending on your location, had become the new normal. Catchphrases like "pivot," "working from home," or, as the younger generation would say, "hashtag WFH," had become part of our everyday vocabulary. Who would have predicted that this time would always be preceded by the word 'unprecedented'? At best, a word that seemed as vaguely effective (and perhaps questionable) as wearing a mask. While our lives might have been confined to our homes for a while, in the hope of containing the virus's further spread, the 'lockdown' had forced the world to pause and reflect. The devastating impact on lives and the economic downturn affecting small businesses and jobs had taken an unbearable and sudden toll. No one saw this coming, and nobody could have truly been prepared for such an immediate halt to life as we knew it.

This enforced pause thrust us into a collective moment of stillness. For some, the workload had only intensified, a reality I had personally experienced. As I sat at my desk, navigating this new way of working, I couldn't help but think about the global timeout that had sent us metaphorically to the bench to catch our breath. Luxuries and conveniences that had once made life simpler had become temporarily out of reach. It's in these moments of quiet reflection that I've come to understand the true value of patience.

In the initial chaos of the pandemic, society's reaction was a frenzied scramble for normalcy. Even the mundane act of buying toilet paper became a trending topic. I remember chuckling at hashtags like #toiletgate, yet there was a deeper, more reflective side to this. It highlighted our collective impatience and desperation for control in uncertain times.

Observing this, I've come to realise that society's natural inclination today is to see patience as a weakness, not a strength. Why wait when everything is just a click away? This question lingered in my mind as I noticed people's frustration over minor delays in their daily lives. Our culture, as I've come to see it, views waiting as oppressive and unfair. This realisation struck a chord with me, as I too have been guilty of impatience, whether in traffic or while waiting for a morning coffee.

My journey through these tumultuous times has led me to explore the concept of patience more deeply. This virtue, once cherished, seems to be fading in our fast-paced world. As I delved into this exploration, I was reminded of a BBC documentary I watched during the pandemic's latter stages, 'The Year the Earth Changed.' It beautifully illustrated the transformative power of slowing down. This notion resonated with me, as I saw nature thrive while humanity paused. It was a profound lesson in the benefits of patience, not just for us but for our planet.

The process of writing this book has been one of learning and embracing patience. The irony is not lost on me that it took losing my job for this book to see the light of day. It's as if the universe conspired to ensure I had the time to reflect and write. And now, here we are, with a book filled with thoughts and ideas. I invite you to journey through these pages at a leisurely pace, just as I learned to do. Take your time to ponder, debate, and, if you're up for it, engage in a full-on conversation with the concepts presented here. There's no need to rush, my friend. Trust me, do as I did and take it one page at a time. You'll be rewarded for your patience.

Part One
Essence of Patience

Divine Timing: Patience from Creation's Beginning

The universe is not in a hurry. You are.

— Unknown

LET'S BEGIN, SHALL WE?

At the very start.

Not just with this chapter but tracing back to the dawn of time itself. Now, rest assured, this won't be a complex expedition through the intricacies of the space-time continuum or an intense dive into quantum physics. Instead, this chapter explores the intriguing intersection of science, theology, and philosophy in understanding the concept of patience, particularly in the context of creation. We will examine how various perspectives, from scientific theories like the Big Bang and cosmic inflation to biblical narratives of divine creation, contribute to our understanding of patience as an integral element in the formation and ongoing evolution of the universe. In doing so, we will unravel whether patience is merely a passive waiting or an active force shaping existence and how this understanding influences our perception of time, creation, and the very essence of life itself.

Stephen Hawking once noted, "Many people do not like the idea that time has a beginning, probably because it smacks of divine intervention."[1] Regardless of which starting point you lean towards, we can agree it converges at a pivotal moment. This raises the curtain on two prominent theories about the universe's origins. On the one hand, the scientific community presents the Big Bang theory, a term coined by Fred Hoyle, to explain a universe that sparked into existence 13.8 billion years ago, eventually leading to the evolution of human life on Earth.[2] On the other hand, the religious community embraces the concept of a divine creator who meticulously crafted the Heavens and Earth, instilling life with a purpose. Despite their differing views, both schools of thought converge on a critical agreement: the universe's inception was not instantaneous.

The scientific perspective suggests a theory predating

---

1. Stephen Hawking, A Brief History of Time (New York: Bantam, 1998) 49.
2. Helge Kragh, Big Bang: the etymology of a name, Astronomy & Geophysics, Volume 54, Issue 2, April 2013, Pages 2.28–2.30, https://doi.org/10.1093/astrogeo/atto35

the Big Bang, called cosmic inflation, indicating a rapid expansion in the timeline more or less within 10^{-32} seconds followed by years of slowing down, but not all together in a flash, as some tend to believe.[3] Similarly, Judeo-Christian teachings acknowledge that creation wasn't an instant act. God didn't simply snap His fingers and voila! Life appeared as quickly as a Big Mac order at a drive-through. There was an order in which the universe and life within it came into being. This coming into existence implies a process. The Greek word for coming into being, "geneseōs," is a derivative of "Genesis." Whether you believe the existence of the Earth came from nothing or a divine designer, you would be hard-pressed to ignore whether life gave birth to the virtue of patience or if life itself is the very result of it.

In 2009, a memorable debate unfolded between William Lane Craig, a respected Christian apologist, and Christopher Hitchens, a prominent atheist writer.[4] Held at Biola University, this engaging exchange drew attention to profound existential questions. During the debate, Craig presented the fine-tuning argument, a cornerstone of his

---

3. Siegel, E, 2019, Forbes Magazine, What Came First: Inflation Or The Big Bang?
4. Does God Exist? William Lane Craig vs. Christopher Hitchens. Biola University, La Mirada, California - April 4, 2009. https://www.youtube.com/watch?v=otYm41hb48o

apologetic approach, suggesting that the universe's precise laws and constants signify the presence of a deliberate Creator. He argued that the improbability of such fine-tuning arising by chance points to a divine hand in the creation process. Hitchens countered this by questioning the need for a creator, emphasising the capacity of natural processes, as understood by modern science, to account for the universe's characteristics. A particularly striking moment came when Hitchens questioned the 'waste' of time in the divine plan of creation, pointing to the billions of years it took for human life to emerge.[5] Craig's response highlighted the theme of patience in creation from a divine perspective. He argued that concerns of efficiency and speed are human constraints and do not apply to a timeless, resource-unlimited divine being.[6] This argument brought to the forefront the concept of divine patience, suggesting that the act of creation, from a theological standpoint, is an enduring process, marked not by haste but by a deliberate and purposeful unfolding. This debate thus encapsulates the central theme of our chapter: the exploration of patience in the context of creation. It juxtaposes the scientific view of a universe that seemingly

---

5. Does God Exist? The Craig-Hitchens Debate. William Lane Craig vs. Christopher Hitchens. Biola University, La Mirada, California - April 4, 2009. https://www.reasonablefaith.org/media/debates/does-god-exist

6. Does God Exist? The Craig-Hitchens Debate. William Lane Craig vs. Christopher Hitchens, Biola University, La Mirada, California - April 4, 2009. https://www.reasonablefaith.org/media/debates/does-god-exist

follows a natural, undirected course, with the theological view that sees a patient and purposeful Creator behind the cosmos. The exchange between Craig and Hitchens offers a vivid illustration of how these differing perspectives shape our understanding of time, existence, and the very nature of patience itself.

Reflecting on the thought-provoking debate, we see a contemporary exploration of divine timing and patience, themes that have resonated throughout history. This brings us to a seminal scriptural account that has long provided insight into these very concepts. The narrative of Genesis 1:1-2:4 in the Bible is not just an ancient story; it epitomises the idea of divine patience and deliberate creation. Just as Craig and Hitchens debated the nature and timing of creation, Genesis offers a profound reflection on these themes, inviting us to consider the meticulous and purposeful process of bringing the universe into existence. The act itself is described as 'letting things unfurl or be'— where God himself moves through a series of motions: He inculcates, oversees, waits and affirms the free biodiversity of flora and fauna. This is, as I mentioned at the beginning of this chapter, the "coming in to being". This act of creating the world out of nothing was given careful consideration from great theological scholars like Augustine. It's often referred to in latin as creatio ex nihilo — attributing God as the responsible author of dynamic, complex and valuable cosmos. Nothing was presupposed. But many theologians held to the belief that creation continues to happen throughout time. Many believed that

God never stopped completely on the seventh day, it was more a pause than a hard stop and His work continues. This was referred to by the early church fathers as preservation.[7] If you think about it like this, life is coming into existence all the time, new species are discovered that never existed before — a prime example of His ongoing work and continual creation. This hypotheses of continuation of God's original work (Creation Continua) was further contended by Thomas Aquinas. He saw time and the universe as a function and measurement of change.[8] He believed that non-human life depended entirely on God's creative act, his efforts of creation included their empowerment who in turn showed loyalty of life to God's patience. I often wonder, if God created the heavens and the earth to manifest humanity in His image, then He displayed enormous patience. If creation is truly continual then creation itself must be the highest form of patience.

I'm reminded of how this principle of patience and continual creation manifests in human endeavours like in Antoni Gaudí's Sagrada Familia in Spain. I had the pleasure of seeing this on a short trip to Barcelona with my brother. Much like the divine process of creation, which we see as an ongoing act transcending time, Gaudí's

---

7. Barber, Bruce and Neville, David. Theodicy and Eschatology. Australia: ATF Press, 2005. Creation and Eschatology: Chia, Raymond, 175.
8. Barber, Bruce and Neville, David. Theodicy and Eschatology. Australia: ATF Press, 2005. Creation and Eschatology: Chia, Raymond, 176.

masterpiece stands as a testament to the human embodiment of patience and perseverance. The construction of the Sagrada Familia has spanned over a century, defying the typical constraints of time and completion. This architectural marvel, still in progress, parallels the concept of continuous creation in its own unique way. The very thought of such an architectural project existing in today's world seems absurd and unheard of. It leads one to ponder if our endeavors, both divine and human, are a reflection of a deeper, timeless patience. Just as the creation of the Heavens and Earth unfolds in a divine rhythm beyond our comprehension, so too does Gaudí's Sagrada Familia rise slowly, stone by stone, towards the heavens. In this light, perhaps the true essence of creation, whether by divine hands or human effort, lies not in the haste of completion but in the enduring patience and dedication that span generations. This enduring commitment challenges us to appreciate the beauty in the process itself, finding meaning in the journey as much as in the finished creation.

As we reflect on the Old Testament narrative of creation, with its emphasis on a methodical and patient unfolding of the universe, we naturally progress to another pivotal moment in divine history: the arrival of Christ as narrated in the New Testament. This event, too, can be seen through the lens of divine timing and patience. Just as the creation narrative in Genesis reveals a deliberate process over days, the arrival of Christ represents another aspect of God's timing in human history. The decision of when to send Christ into the world wasn't arbitrary but was perfectly aligned with a broader divine plan. Theologians and scholars, like William Lane Craig, have pondered why this momentous event occurred when it did, considering the cultural, historical, and spiritual readiness of humanity at that time. "The timing of this event was not just about the span of years but also about the readiness of humanity and the world: The population reference bureau estimates that the number of people who have ever lived on this planet is about a hundred and five billion people. Only two percent of them were born prior to the advent of Christ. Erik Kreps of the Survey Research Center of the University of Michigan's Institute for social research says, "Gods's timing couldn't have been more perfect. Christ showed up just before the exponential explosion in the world's population".[9] Craig continues, "The bible says in the fullness of time God sent forth his son and when Christ came the nation of Israel had been prepared; the Roman peace dominated the Mediterranean world; it was an age of literacy and learning; the stage was set for the advent of God's son into the world and I think in God's providential plan for human history we see the wisdom of

---

9. Erik Kreps quoted in Dinesh D'Souza, *What's So Great About Christianity?* (Wheaton, IL: Tyndale, 2007), p. 64.

God orchestrating the development human life and then in bringing Christ into the world in fullness of time". [10]

This perspective on divine timing resonates with the biblical narrative of Christ's second coming. In 2 Peter the apostle urges the church in Asia to be patient, despite an undercurrent of impatience boiling up amongst false teachers. Again, you could imagine someone like Hitchens standing up and saying, "What's with the delay? They questioned God's timing and doubted His Word in taking so long with Christ's return. But Peter responds to this delay in an almost poetic quip that sounds like it could equally have come from the wisdom of Yoda, "...a single day is like a thousand years with the Lord and a thousand years are like a single day" (2 Peter 3:8 NET). What's interesting is that preceding this verse the apostle Peter uses creation to illustrate God's timing since the beginning of time itself, but then bookends the second paragraph by pointing to the new Heavens and new Earth. This will be the fullness of new creation. Later in verse 15 he urges the church to regard God's patience as salvation. The whole point of God's long-suffering is He's offering the world, even to this day, an opportunity to repent. If this isn't enough evidence of His desire for us to not perish then we have missed the point of His love for the world completely.

---

10. Does God Exist? The Craig-Hitchens Debate. William Lane Craig vs. Christopher Hitchens, Biola University, La Mirada, California - April 4, 2009. https://www.reasonablefaith.org/media/debates/does-god-exist

12 Peeling an Orange

Having explored the divine timing in the historical context of Christ's arrival, we now turn to another dimension of this theme as articulated by the apostles, particularly Peter. In his letters, Peter addresses the concept of divine patience and timing, not only in historical events but also in the unfolding of God's plan for humanity. This perspective is especially evident in 2 Peter, where the apostle reflects on the nature of time from a divine viewpoint. Was he being literal in saying one day is like a thousand years? We know he used the simile 'like' rather than using 'is'. Then there are those that think days is far too long for a God who is omnipotent, infinite: possessing infinite power, knowledge, wisdom, to create anything He so desired at the snap of His fingers and be done with it. The whole universe, the earth and all living life on it. If we accept that days refer to as ordinary days, we understand that God is telling us that it took Him this amount of days to work and one day to rest, setting a pattern for man to live by — the pattern of the seven day week, one of those of which we rest, along with Saturday of course, unless you're Tim Ferris and only work a 4-hour work week.[11] God is illustrating the six days of work, to stop and take stock on the seventh. The six days are juxtaposed to the seventh.

---

11. Ferriss, Timothy. 2009. *The 4-Hour Workweek: Escape 9-5, Live Anywhere, and Join the New Rich* Expanded and Updated ed., 1st revised ed. New York: Crown.

The creation days are emblematic of God's word which finished on the sixth day. The seventh wasn't a result of exhaustion, but a pause from creating. Within the work itself, like anything, are moments of patience, of things playing out over a period of time that cannot be rushed, nor skipped to move on to the next stage. There's almost a methodical process of the divine. The Sabbath is a callout to humanity to do the same, but more profoundly it personifies the rest that is ultimately found in the person of Christ. Jesus tells us in Matthew 11:28 to seek him and find solace. Apart from the intention of rest, when you take a closer look at the six days it's evident of a pattern rather than some random tradition many see it as today. It's a reference of "taking time"— of laying out a systematic order of things. General to more complex as God designed an ecosystem that would thrive on earth. Could it be that within this period of a week as we refer to it now, that God was being patient in putting things in coherent order, over periods of time, so that it could not only be recorded by Moses and relayed over thousands of years, but also so humanity could see a logic, power and wisdom unfolding all wrapped within the patience of God's creation? And we see creations timeline referenced after Genesis in Exodus 31:18. The fourth commandment, in verse 9 of chapter 20, tells us that we are to work for six days and rest for one. The justification for this is given in verse 11: "For in six days the Lord made heaven and earth, the sea, and all that in them is, and rested the seventh day; wherefore the Lord blessed the sabbath day, and hallowed it."

Perhaps this logic prevents a discourse of free will as sin entered the world before Adam and Eve in the garden, but we also know sin is contrary to the nature of God. So was this order part of the plan? Furthermore, theories abound that the number seven connotes to completeness or wholeness. We also see this number referenced throughout the bible. If any of these theories hold true, and if God truly demonstrated such a deliberate and patient approach in creating the universe, then it stands to reason that we would find a consistent pattern of patience woven throughout the Bible. This pattern would reveal how time is carefully stretched across the ages, reflecting the same enduring temperament toward a world that persistently resists and disobeys Him. After all, it took roughly four thousand years from the birth of Adam to Christ. That's a long time for God to sit it out and redeem the world and of course, annoy atheists like Hitchens.

As we explore these themes further, it becomes apparent that the concept of patience is woven throughout both the Old and New Testament. This consistent theme is not just a historical or theological construct but a practical guide for living. It encourages us to find joy in God's timing, to embrace the rhythm of life He has set, and to trust in the unfolding of His greater plan. This journey through the chapters of patience in our lives reveals that waiting, when done with faith and expectation, can lead to profound blessings and deeper understanding. As we continue this journey, we're reminded of God's enduring patience, not just as a historical fact but as a living reality. It teaches us to see patience not as a burden but as a virtue, urging us to view waiting as an opportunity for growth and transformation. In this way, God's patience from creation becomes a source of strength and inspiration, guiding us through life's ups and downs with a promise of something greater to come.

Virtues of Patience

We applaud patience, but prefer it to be a virtue that others possess.

— NT Wright

AS A CHILD A PROVERBIAL PHRASE ADORNED MY bedroom door: "Good things come to those who wait." Centred on cardboard laminate, its corners bore circular stains from constant reapplication of blue-tack. I had discovered this phrase at a local Christian bookstore, a stark contrast to my mother's purchase of a silver acrylic fish for her Volkswagen Jetta's bumper, a silent testament so those behind her knew where she was eternally headed. I naively believed the phrase might have biblical origins, not realising its absence of direct scriptural reference.

Such phrases, like 'All Good things come to those who wait' or 'Let sleeping dogs lie,' often roll off our tongues without much thought about their origins or meanings. This curiosity led me to explore the historical roots of these sayings, particularly the well–known adage, 'Patience is a virtue.' A phrase, often uttered in moments of haste or frustration, has a rich history dating back to the Middle Ages. It is attributed to William Langland's, 'The Vision of Piers Plowman,' a work which delves into the essence of true Christianity through allegorical storytelling.[1] In this poem, Langland grapples with the four cardinal virtues, including temperance (or patience) — the virtue tied to fortitude and the ability to endure pain or adversity. However, identifying this in the original text is challenging because it was written in an English that differs greatly from what we use today. Understanding the Middle English version is as difficult as deciphering the slurred speech of someone who's had too much to drink:

> *Why I suffre or noght suffre--thiself hast*
>   *noght to doone.*   11.376
> *Amende thow it if thow myght, for my tyme*
>   *is to abide.*   11.377
> *Suffraunce is a soverayn vertue, and a swift*
>   *vengeaunce.*   11.378

---

1. Economou, George., Langland, William. William Langland's "Piers Plowman": The C Version. United States: University of Pennsylvania Press, Incorporated, 1996, 209.

> *Who suffreth moore than God?' quod he;*
> *"no gome, as I leeve.*   11.379
> *He myghte amende in a minute while al*
> *that mysstandeth,*   11.380
> *Ac he suffreth for som mannes goode, ad so*
> *is oure bettre.*

Some of these words might seem like an Elvish dialect straight out of a Tolkien novel, but with enough time and focus, you can start to decipher their meaning as certain words begin to emerge in clear English. This phenomenon, where our brains can still recognise words despite the jumbled letters, is known as 'Typoglycaemia,' or the transposed letter effect.[2] For instance, the line "Suffraunce is a soverayn vertue" translates to 'Patience is a (supreme or good) virtue.' We don't often attribute the word suffering with patience, only the emotion experienced because of it. This translation reveals that patience, derived from the Latin verb 'pati' meaning to suffer, is more than simply waiting; it involves enduring with hope and resilience. Suffer in a sense isn't immediately negative, much like the word endurance is. Joy can be found in enduring. The Bible often references patience as 'long-suffering' or 'sufferance.' This theme of patience as a moral and virtuous quality resonates beyond Langland's work, finding echoes in other literary masterpieces. For example,

---

2. https://en.wikipedia.org/wiki/Transposed_letter_effect#Internet_meme

Geoffrey Chaucer, in 'The Canterbury Tales,' echoes this sentiment by noting, 'Patience is a great virtue of perfection.' Such literary works collectively underscore patience's esteemed place in human character, depicting it as a crucial trait for navigating life's complexities and challenges. This literary tradition, extending from Langland to Chaucer and beyond, illustrates how patience has been revered and reflected upon through the ages, influencing philosophical thought and shaping cultural narratives. In the end, an exploration reveals that the simple phrases of our childhood often carry a weighty historical and ethical significance.

The exploration of patience in literary works, where it often determines the fates of characters, naturally leads us to consider how this virtue is depicted in other narrative forms, particularly in biblical texts. One of the most profound examples of patience can be found in the Bible, a source of moral and ethical guidance for many. The story of the Israelites' journey to the Promised Land is a classic biblical narrative that exemplifies patience in a spiritual context. Their whole journey is a labour intensive test of patience. No other people had the world thrown at them as much as they did. Their story is a testament to enduring faith, as detailed in Hebrews 11. You only need to read how some of them kept their faith till their deathbed, if that isn't an exercise of patience I'm not sure what is. Of course if we were to look for the word literally, the only time it appears is in Nehemiah 9:30 and Jeremiah 15. Notably in both instances it's a reference to God's patience, which is equally a big part of the story, and I hope to get to unpack a little later in the book. Even so, we can see the theme equally in all the verses mentioned above — the evidential importance of the future joy and rewards that awaits as a result of practicing this virtue. Patience becomes a little more obvious and explicitly mentioned as we crossover into the New Testament. The first that comes to mind is the Apostle Paul's letter to the Church of Corinth about love. In what I call the "wedding favourite", it's the first thing he celebrates in Chapter 1 Corinthians 13:14 — "Love is patient". Now it doesn't explicitly say it's a virtue, but if we read it in the context of the passage we can see that is read to be a virtue because everything preceding and aforementioned is about the way of love and how Paul is emphasising the importance of this for the church. Notice how everything following this verse are things that are often quick knee-jerk reactions, anger, irritability, arrogance, and envy. All emotions that are often our first response, right? Someone cuts in front of us, or rocks up to a barbecue in their flash new car. What is our immediate reaction? Is it love? Or are we to practice this virtue so that through slowing our response down, through being patient we might take a step back and allow love to rise to the top. We also see this mentioned by Paul in Galatians 5-22:23 when he's referencing patience as fruit of the Spirit. We know the fruit of the Spirit is love, joy, peace, forbearance, kindness, goodness, faithfulness, gentleness and self-control. Against such things there is no law. What's interesting about this verse and the one above is that in some instances in the bible patience is always coupled with other virtues.

The narrative of the Israelites, laden with trials and a test of collective patience, sets the stage for another pivotal manifestation of this virtue within the Bible: the life and teachings of Jesus Christ. In the New Testament, Christ's embodiment of patience marks a significant shift in how this virtue is understood and practiced. His life, as narrated in the Gospels, provides numerous instances where patience is not just a passive endurance but an active expression of love, compassion, and wisdom. From patiently teaching His disciples to showing forbearance towards those in need, Christ's actions offer a deeper insight into the multifaceted nature of patience. Christ's approach to challenging situations was always grounded in love and compassion, demonstrating that patience is foundational to a multitude of virtues. It would certainly be impossible to show patience without a deep love for people. A hardened heart is like a hammer, you begin to see everything around you as a nail. Not to misappropriate Maslow's quote, but my point is this, when you heart is to hard to show love, anger is always solely the behavioural repercussion. Whereas love, as seen through Christ, opens up to a multitude of virtues. From love we must find our way to patience, for it is the nucleus to laying a foundation for slowing down anger, and leading with what stems from patience: compassion, understanding, tranquility, gratitude, generosity and mindfulness. This transition from the Old Testament's emphasis on patience as a communal journey of faith to the New Testament's focus on Christ's personal example offers a comprehensive biblical view of this virtue, enriching our understanding of its significance in both personal and collective contexts.

Having seen how Christ exemplified patience through his life and teachings, we are now better positioned to understand the broader implications of this virtue in our daily lives. This perspective is crucially expanded upon by contemporary writers like James S. Spiegel. In his book 'How to Be Good in a World Gone Bad: Living a Life of Christian Virtue,' Spiegel delves into the concept of patience, not just as an isolated virtue but as a composite of several qualities like self-control, humility, and generosity. In other words patience is often part of a dynamic family that all have similar attributes. In a sense patience is a virtue because it's a pursuit of a handful of other virtues. When we initially read 1 Corinthians all those attributes were still offshoots of what it means to lack patience. The same is for Galatians, you cannot have self-control or humility unless you harbour a degree of patience. We see it again in Ecclesiastes 7:8 — patience is the companion of humility and the enemy of pride. "The patient in spirit is better than the proud in spirit". So when we look at an attribute like self-control, I for one know I cannot show self control when my wife brings chocolate home, because I immediately rush to unwrap the shiny treat and scoff what I can as quickly as I can before any guilt or common sense settles. Patience has to take the lead. If I don't pause, think about the end result and commit to moderation, or no chocolate at all, I cannot show self-control. Spiegel defines patience as not just waiting without complaint, but to endure discomfort without complaint. Patience is not about seeing through the waiting, but rather enduring that point where you're wrestling with that which is tugging at you demanding you take immediate action, but you're doing so with no groans or moans.

It's clear that when things get uncomfortable or challenging in life, the virtue of patience allows you to deal with discomfort in way that is calm and considered towards the people and situations around you. It's the highest form of exercising self-control and in short, exhibiting such a virtue demonstrates your high moral standard in life. From a Christian perspective there's no disputing patience is a virtue which should be part of our constitution. The daily life God gives us is designed to build virtue in us and patience is the virtue gained through the difficulties and challenges. In doing so, we grow morally, improving in virtue regardless of whether we consider some experiences to be morally relevant, much less meaningful. As Christians we shouldn't be surprised by the building of this virtue in the most unexpected ways, because God is always at work in us. It's a virtue that is equally important as much as it is trying, requiring perseverance and faith, especially in difficult moments. The two go hand in hand together. With every day that dawns so too will our patience be tested, but we can take comfort in these challenges that God remains at work within us. This is not to say we should remain idle in our response to daily difficulties, but prepare our minds and hearts to respond in a Christ-like manner. There is always action in this virtue. Peter reminds us to "prepare your minds for action and self-control" (1 Peter 1:13 NLT). This virtue is not a given, but we must be intentional and disciplined as Christ calls us to be. Unlocking God's will by imitating him in all things, no matter how big or small (Philippians 4:8). While the virtue of patience is commonly associated with conforming oneself with the ability to wait for things, conversely it doesn't always require us to be passive but rather play an active and cognitive role. Perhaps the true state of this virtue requires wisdom in understanding there's empowerment to be found in both.

The Spectrum of Patience: From Stillness to Action

Patience is not passive, on the contrary, it is concentrated strength.

— Bruce Lee

In the small, market town of Alnwick, Northumberland, Stuart Manley, along with his wife Mary, ran a charming secondhand bookstore. Known for its eclectic mix of books, cozy armchairs, a model train set, and a quaint café, it was a true haven for book lovers. One day, while sorting through a box of books from an auction, Stuart stumbled upon an original *Keep Calm and Carry*

On poster.[1] This iconic poster, created by the Ministry of Information during 27 June to 6 July 1939, was part of a morale-boosting series during World War II, designed to fortify the British spirit against potential wartime disasters. Despite its questionable effectiveness back then, the dusty poster hadn't seen the light of day until the couple framed it and hung it up above their cash register. For no other reason than it looked better up than down. This rediscovery led to its global popularisation, embedding itself in modern culture and adorning everything from coffee cups to mouse pads. Its message became an emblem of British resilience, a call to stoicism and calmness in the face of adversity.

The rediscovery of composure and patience highlights their timeless significance, especially in situations beyond our control. During World War II, the British public, living under the imminent threat of invasion and the iconic slogan *Keep Calm and Carry On*, embodied these virtues. In moments where action appears futile, patience and calmness emerge as the most potent responses. While our instincts urge us to rectify problems, true patience often entails refraining from action. Patience manifests in two forms: passive and active. Passive patience involves accepting our limitations, akin to the post-exam period where outcomes are beyond our influence. In contrast, active patience entails steadfast perseverance toward a

---

[1]. "Keep calm and carry on." — British Government, 1939 motivational poster

goal, resembling a soldier's relentless march toward victory.

In scenarios where control eludes us or the timing feels off, we are reminded to maintain our composure. Our daily challenges seem trivial compared to the stakes of a global war. Imagine encountering the *Keep Calm and Carry On* slogan while your city teeters on the brink of invasion. If the Ministry of Defence tweeted a plea for public patience amid imminent danger, the instinct to seek immediate shelter would be overwhelming. For millions of Britons, calmness was their sole defense; there was nowhere else to flee and nothing more they could do. This principle of patience transcends historical contexts, infiltrating our daily lives and relationships. Whether passive or active, patience remains a crucial virtue, guiding us through both monumental and mundane challenges. This was notably evident during a personal experience at a family picnic.

One Sunday afternoon my wife and I were invited by a couple we had grown close with to a family picnic at our local beach. It's a popular bay for families because the water is statue still — the shore faces north east and is sheltered from ocean swell. It's perfect for families, in particular swimming. On any given morning you can find a group of early rises known as the *swimming idiots*. Their comical name is associated with their balmy one kilometre morning swim come rain or shine, without fail. Although swimming wasn't on our agenda the sunny winter afternoon made for perfect picnic conditions under a potbellied oak tree overlooking the bay. We unpacked our mats and food and Adrian and I decided to leave our wives to chat while we took our kids along the the promenade to burn off some energy on their scooter and push bikes. We talked about life and how strange it was at the moment and how oblivious our kids seem to be to the world's worries. Adrian and his wife Clare had recently adopted a beautiful boy who got on so well with my daughter, we often joked by calling each other the *in-laws*. They are amazing parents and I was intrigued to understand what it was like going through the whole ordeal. Not just adoption, but the whole process leading up to it all. The trying for a child, the waiting, the myriad of tests, the back and forth visits to the OB/GYN, the ups and downs of hopeful waiting and eventual disappointments. Then opening your hearts and minds to a new avenue of adoption having only to wait even longer in finding out if you've been accepted or not. Once you're deemed suitable then the lengthly and legal process begins. And, more waiting. So I asked Him.

"How did you manage to remain patient through everything you've recently gone through?"

He stopped and I carried on only to realise he wasn't alongside me. As I turned to look for him he answered in time with his walking again.

"A lot of people think patience is this linear thing. Sometimes it's more of a process. It's not so much about

The Spectrum of Patience: From Stillness to Action   29

what you want and then how do you go about getting it. And...it's not always an A to B kind of thing."

"So then it wasn't so much about waiting for you?", I said.

"Correct!", He chimed, "It's an evolutionary process... it's still ongoing."

"What do you mean ongoing?", I asked

"I'll get to that", I could tell he was reliving every moment of his journey which was clearly something that hadn't quite ended, despite his beautiful boy happily riding his pushbike in front of us. He continued.

"Let me ask you something do you see waiting and patience as the same thing?"

"No, I see it as part of patience", I said.

"Yea, but you see for me waiting is different" he paused, "You're waiting for a result, for something to happen, to come true or to receive some information before taking that next step. Anyone can wait, and sometimes you don't have a choice. So then, is that waiting?"

I wasn't sure if that was rhetorical, so I waited.

"Patience is the characteristic during the process of waiting. You know, because patience produces all these responses and behaviours that you learn about yourself, about life, about love, about different situations you find yourself in."

"It sounds to me patience is often learned through hindsight."

"True", he responded. "When you're in the moment you're wrestling through what that looks like for you. In our case waiting wasn't this passive thing where we just took a backseat in life's waiting room hoping our number would appear on the digital screen signalling our turn. It was active because we were constantly adapting to and changing—working through all these immense highs and lows."

Adrian looked on to his son weaving through the Sunday strollers along the promenade. I could see from the expression on his face how his mind was somewhere else reliving all that he gone through to this point.

"We had to learn to be okay with whatever the result was. That part was passive, the process of waiting I suppose. Learning to be patient even in that moment of knowing we would have a child or not having one and then once having him, only to be left with an even bigger existential question of whether this finally satisfied our need as couple. Has it truly answered our internal desires and questions?"

"So there was another part to it... of patience?", I asked.

"Very much so", he continued. "We still have to deal with patience in that, like keeping in contact with his paternal mother and father and the different siblings that are all out there. These are all new challenges that spawn new circumstances where our patience is constantly put to the test."

His story revealed that patience is more than just waiting; it's an evolving process. For a couple who had spent years waiting to be parents, trying every means possible they finally received a gift which has brought them endless joy and happiness in their lives. From what seemed on the outside like a linear approach of waiting to not waiting anymore, their patience was ever evolving, moving between a passive state to an active one. It was clear that God was continuing to teach them the true virtue of patience and His timing played a crucial role. As the day at the beach drew to a close and I walked away, Adrian's insights lingered in my mind, prompting deeper contemplation on the multifaceted nature of patience and its significant impact on our everyday lives.

This realisation shifted my understanding of patience. Patience isn't just a simple, linear progression from waiting to not waiting; it's a dynamic interplay between active engagement and passive acceptance. After hearing Adrian's story I started to realise the distinction between active and passive patience and the role each had to play. Passive (inactive) patience simply waits it out hoping something will happen. Active patience systematically works towards the end goal. Although patience is the ability to accept or tolerate delay without complaint or suffering, it certainly doesn't mean you always need to stop completely in your tracks. Sometimes things might be out of our control where nothing we can actively do will speed up the process, yet it doesn't imply idle laziness. If you think about it in the context of what happened in the world over the last two years of navigating the pandemic, you can attribute varying degrees of active and passive patience.

Passive patience is being told to stay at home and remain from socialising. Now although life might seem suddenly impotent and stifling there is still passive momentum. Think about it like this, by being patient and not going out I'm playing my bit in helping to bring down the number of Covid cases. I'm also learning to adapt, what we now call the *new normal*. I'm not only learning about myself, but I am applying new habits and perhaps improving on areas I neglected in the past. In other words, I'm seeing my family more and thinking of new ways to interact with them. Now active patience in a situation like this would mean making sure I got double vaccinated over a period of time and actively ensured I ate healthy and kept fit at all times while remaining vigilant in every situation. Although I'm being patient, I'm certainly not doing nothing. I'm pushing forward in the very present until something manifests and there's a breakthrough. Nouwen, a renowned Dutch Catholic priest, professor, writer and theologian, encapsulates this best:

> "Patience is a hard discipline. It is not just waiting until something happens over which we have no control: the arrival of the bus, the end of the rain, the return of a friend, the resolution of a conflict. Patience is not a waiting passivity until someone else does something. Patience asks us to live the moment to the fullest, to be completely present to the moment, to taste the here and now, to be where we are. When we are impatient we try to get away from where we are. We behave as if the real

thing will happen tomorrow, later and somewhere else. Let's be patient and trust that the treasure we look for is hidden in the ground on which we stand."[2]

Much like the call to the British public during World War II, this is the manifesto of Keep Calm and Carry On. As Tolstoy once said, "but to keep going when the going is hard and slow — that is patience. The two most powerful warriors are patience and time."[3]

The exploration of patience in personal contexts naturally extends into the realm of spiritual life, particularly within Christian settings and teachings. If you frequently mix in Christian circles you would most likely either have heard or repeated the the familiar platitude of *waiting on the Lord*. "I'm waiting on the Lord to guide me to my next job", "I'm waiting on the Lord to know if she'll be my wife", "I'm waiting on the Lord to heal me". Admittedly, there are times this phrase has become throw away and lost it's gravity. To *wait on the Lord* isn't idle resting. Although elements of it might be passive, it's in intent often requiring fervent intercession and time spent within the scriptures. A friend of mine would often try to be patient in hearing from God first before making any next step, but this often meant little to no action on his part. While divine guidance provides a roadmap to know the right

---

2. Nouwen, Henri J. M.. Bread for the Journey: A Daybook of Wisdom and Faith. United States: HarperCollins, 2009, page 5
3. Leo Tolstoy, *War and Peace*, Book Ten, 1812.

direction to take for a godly life, a docked ship will also never get you anywhere until you set sail. God never stops giving direction even when you feel like you are't equipped to go anywhere. When Jesus told his disciples to wait for the Holy Spirit and only then go forth and witness to the world (Acts 1:4-8), he didn't mean for them to sit around do nothing. Waiting for the coming of the kingdom isn't inactivity, but moving in the Spirit under the authority of the Father who has appointed a time and season for everything. Jesus would urge his anxious disciples to remain patient upon the Father, just as the Lord did. And Jesus lead by example, passionately waiting on His Father while actively pursuing His will. If he had been impatient, or unwilling to seek His Father's will and obey his timing, there would never have been the greatest sacrifice off all. With no crucifixion we wouldn't have the gift of the resurrection. And with no resurrection God's promise of a new earth would not be fulfilled. His pursuit was very much active, acting in God's will and fulfilling all righteousness that we might be accounted righteous in Him. We have the choice to simply inhabit the earth and wait for Christ's return, or we can act out a faith that sees his Kingdom manifested on earth by having an impact on the world in which we live. James, in his epistle, urges believers to be patient like farmers awaiting the harvest in 5:7-12:

> "Be patient, then, brothers and sisters, until the Lord's coming. See how the farmer waits for the land to yield its

valuable crop, patiently waiting for the autumn and spring rains. You too, be patient and stand firm, because the Lord's coming is near. Don't grumble against one another, brothers and sisters, or you will be judged. The Judge is standing at the door!"

"Brothers and sisters, as an example of patience in the face of suffering, take the prophets who spoke in the name of the Lord. As you know, we count as blessed those who have persevered. You have heard of Job's perseverance and have seen what the Lord finally brought about. The Lord is full of compassion and mercy."

His patience isn't passive but involves diligent work and preparation. It's a reminder that our actions today contribute to a future shaped by our faith and perseverance.

This understanding of patience, both in personal experiences and spiritual teachings, brings us full circle to the essence of the Keep Calm and Carry On message. Patience whether it manifests as active engagement or passive endurance, is in all its forms a vital aspect of our lives. It teaches us to navigate the complexities of life with hope and resilience, trusting in God's timing and plan. As we face each day, we are called to practice patience, actively engaging with our circumstances while holding onto the promise of a better tomorrow.

Waiting Well

Waiting on God requires the willingness to bear uncertainty, to carry within oneself the unanswered question, lifting the heart to God about it whenever it intrudes upon one's thoughts.

— Elisabeth Elliot.

IN THE 1960s, WALSTER MISCHEL, A PROFESSOR AT Stanford University began a modest experiment of delayed gratification testing the self-restraint of four-year-old children — the ability to abstain from instant, but less-desirable results in favour of varied but more-desirable outcomes.[1] He placed preschool children alone at a table

---

1. Mischel W, Ebbesen EB, Zeiss AR. Cognitive and attentional mech-

with a marshmallow. The campsite favourite of sugar spongey sweetness. Before leaving them with the desired treat, he offered them a choice: either ring a bell and, in doing so, summon the researcher back so they could eat the marshmallow or wait until the researcher spontaneously returned and be rewarded with two marshmallows instead. At the same time, the use of a marshmallow seemed trivial. In theory, it was significant to the desires of the children. This would be apparent once he left the room and observed their actions behind a two-way glass room, eagerly waiting like a detective looking for answers. What he noticed in some of the children was an overwhelming desire inhabiting their ability to wait a full minute, causing them to relent and immediately eat the marshmallow. With the few who were able to stay, he noticed something remarkable. Each child executed various techniques to offer momentary distraction: hands over their eyes, sitting on their hands, singing, fiddling, turning around in their chairs, anything but focussing on the treat before them. Only thirty per cent of the 'high delayers' could wait and stave off temptation, while the 'low delayers' relented. As the study progressed, he tried to impart various behavioural tactics to help outlast the desire, like getting them to think of the marshmallows as something else, for instance, a cotton ball. This helped

---

anisms in delay of gratification. J Pers Soc Psychol. 1972 Feb;21(2):204-18. doi: 10.1037/h0032198. PMID: 5010404.

shift their mindset, resulting in better results, but it needed to be more foolproof.

Interestingly enough he followed up with the children years later into their adult life and made some profound correlations and observations. The children who originally delayed gratification longer achieved better academic results, health, and relationships. This was huge at the time because what it revealed is self-control can be learned, as well as practiced and that doing so at an early age means you'll be able to apply restraint later within all sorts of life challenges. Mischel referred to it as a "protective buffer against the development of all kids of vulnerabilities later in life". Proof that having the ability to wait can have a dramatic impact within challenging areas of your life.

Taking a closer look at how this plays out in our daily lives, the insightful revelations of Mischel's marshmallow experiment resonate profoundly. It's fascinating how those children's decision to wait or not for that extra marshmallow mirrors our daily struggles and triumphs with patience. Every time we're counting down the minutes for something small or oversized, we're living our version of that experiment, juggling between immediate desires and the rewards of holding off just a bit longer. So why is it so hard to wait even when we might know certain things in advance? We can all relate as children to how hard waiting was on Christmas Eve. The anticipation for morning light followed with leaping out of bed and excitedly dancing to the foot of the Christmas tree. But not all waiting, despite knowing the outcome, is always filled with childlike jubilation. Waiting can be tedious whether we wish to prolong it or not. And it's part of our everyday.

A typical day for me starts with waiting for my alarm to go off, the kettle to boil, and the shower stream to warm up. I'm still waiting for my daughter to lie so I can change her. I was waiting in traffic to get her to daycare, for responses to emails, and for a meeting to start. I was waiting in line to order lunch and so on. Each day is punctuated by moments of waiting, existing within a timeframe from initiation to the event's occurrence. The act of waiting, by definition, involves delaying action until a specific event happens. Most often, this delay is beyond our control.

These daily instances of waiting, whether trivial or significant, highlight a larger truth about human behaviour — the innate capacity to transform mere waiting into the art of patience. Psychologists suggest that humans have the capacity to transform waiting into patience.[2] Patience, contrary to being merely the ability to wait, can be influenced positively or negatively by our mindset. At times, after exhausting all options, all that remains is patience. I recall a staff member under my management who was eager for a promotion despite lacking in experience. She was on the right path, but her timing was off. I encouraged

---

2. Bandak, Andreas, and Mette K. Janeja. "Introduction: Worth the Wait." In *The Power of Waiting: Doubt, Hope, and Uncertainty*, 1-18. OAPEN Library, 2018. https://library.oapen.org/bitstream/handle/20.500.12657/43482/external_content.pdf#page=18.

her to shift her focus from the hourglass to her development, reassuring her that her time would come. If she could transform her waiting into patience, the reward would eventually follow. In the book Outliers, Malcolm Gladwell draws an analogy between masters of their craft and time spent learning and practicing.[3] Mozart didn't produce his greatest work until he had been composing for more than twenty years and chess grandmaster, Bobby Fischer took almost ten years of practice before even reaching elite level. These are just two examples of many more who fostered patience for a particular goal or success.

Reflecting on these psychological insights, I am reminded of my own experiences where patience, or the lack thereof, played a pivotal role. Waiting can become a burdensome weight, especially when it skews our present mindset with anticipation for the future. This constant state of anticipation can be overwhelming, but we can choose the tense in which to live. Instead of watching paint dry, put down the brush and walk away. Reflecting on my time in London, my eagerness for a career breakthrough made my waiting burdensome, overshadowing the opportunity for positive growth during that period. Humans often exhibit a commission bias, preferring action over inaction. However,

---

3. Gladwell, Malcolm. Outliers: The Story of Success. United Kingdom: Penguin Books Limited, 2008.

sometimes the best course is to let things unfold in their own time.

My journey in London, punctuated by periods of eager waiting, mirrors a universal human tendency to grapple with the balance between waiting and acting. In moments of waiting where patience is required, whether delaying an action or slowly moving forwards, it's important to distinguish the difference between the two. Waiting is not an attitude. Waiting merely brings out certain emotions. When I look back to my time in London waiting for a career break instead of fostering a positive attitude of patience didn't get me to where I wanted to be any quicker. No matter how hard I tried I couldn't speed up time to be on parity with my housemates. It often felt slow and constant. My experience of life in London was marred by heaviness because my waiting became my ultimate burden and this burden became my obstacle in accepting a delay suffocating any remaining pockets of positive attitude. I felt crushed by the weight of my own impatience left in a state of proverbial purgatory. It was if I was living on a mezzanine floor with no clear entry point to the next level up. Anyone would be exhausted from all the pacing up and down. Little did I know that slowly processing and exercising patience is the first step in avoiding anxiety of the state of delay.

This internal struggle between waiting and action aligns with what behavioural scientists term 'commission bias' — the inclination to favour action over inaction, even when patience might be the wiser course. If we don't see results, we get impatient and feel a strong urge to do something, anything to expedite our progress. But often the best thing we can do is nothing — staying the course, tweaking as we go, and letting things unfold in their own time. Instead of always thinking, "Don't just stand there, do something", we should at least consider thinking, "Don't just do something, stand there."[4]

The other way is by letting go of any preconceived expectations. Patience can often accompany waiting rather than being mutually exclusive or at odds with it. By letting go of preconceived expectations and being intentional about how you act while waiting, your attitude can transform the experience. This shift in mindset can relieve the burden of waiting, making it less cumbersome. In other words, you are letting go but are also intentional about your actions during that time. Your attitude is what converts waiting into patience. This concept is similar to the delayed gratification experiment, where children who waited and demonstrated patience were rewarded with two marshmallows. Patience needs to be fostered from an

---

4. Stulberg, Brand, September 8, The Secret to Success? Mastering the Art of Patience. TIME MAGAZINE 2021, https://time.com/6095843/learning-patience/

early age; otherwise, waiting may remain a burden, leading to frustration and anxiety.

This dichotomy between passive waiting and proactive abiding finds a fascinating parallel in one of my favourite movies of all time, *The Big Lebowski*. The film's portrayal of 'Dudeism' or 'abiding' presents a stark contrast between merely waiting and actively abiding in Christ. Unlike the laid-back ethos of The Dude, abiding in Christ demands a profound trust and acceptance of all that God offers through Him. It is about welcoming and trusting Christ deeply, inviting Him into the very core of our being. It is akin to savouring a delicious meal, but instead, we are savouring the essence of Jesus.

In John 6:35, Jesus declares, "I am the bread of life; whoever comes to me shall not hunger, and whoever believes in me shall never thirst." This statement encapsulates the essence of abiding – a promise of spiritual nourishment and fulfilment. Furthermore, in John 15:7, Jesus emphasises, "If you abide in me, and my words abide in you, ask whatever you wish, and it will be done for you." Here, abiding is depicted as an intimate relationship with Christ, where His words become part of our very being, shaping our desires and actions.

Jesus continues in John 15:9, "As the Father has loved me, so have I loved you. Abide in my love." This love is not passive but an active engagement with Christ's presence, a continual dwelling in His love. Abiding reveals whether we are genuinely connected to the vine, with life coursing through our veins, or if our faith is superficial. As John 15:8 states, "By this, my Father is glorified, that you bear much fruit and so prove to be my disciples." The fruit we bear through abiding is the tangible proof of our discipleship, the evidence of a life deeply rooted in Christ.

Thus, abiding in Christ is not a passive state but a dynamic, life-giving relationship. It is the profound act of dwelling in His presence, receiving His sustenance, and allowing His life to flow through us, transforming us and bearing witness to our true identity as His disciples.

Resilient Living: Endurance and Perseverance in Practice

It's not that I'm so smart, it's just that I stay with problems longer

— Albert Einstein

Endurance is the crowning quality, And patience all the passion of great hearts

— James Russell Lowell.

IF THERE'S ONE THING THE CORONAVIRUS PANDEMIC has reinforced, it's the ability to live in confined spaces without succumbing to cabin fever. Despite having life's necessities and luxuries, including Netflix and the constant hum of the refrigerator, there were moments when these comforts felt overwhelming, leaving me yearning for simpler times before the word 'unprecedented' became a cliché.

In these times, where our own homes felt like a confinement, I found a peculiar kinship in 'Above the Below,' a documentary on David Blaine's extraordinary act of self-confinement. His endurance act of forty-four days in a suspended plexiglass box thirty feet in the air was a stark reminder of the human capacity to endure extreme conditions. It was reported that "during the stunt Blaine was harassed by the British public, "pelting him with eggs, and paint-filled balloons. Golf balls were struck in his direction from Tower Bridge".[1] One prankster even flew a hamburger attached to a remote control helicopter right up to the box to taunt the starving artist. Blaine was nonplussed and took the concept of patience to an extreme, "... to the *purest state you can be in*", reminiscent of biblical figures like Moses. His feat, though primarily a performance art piece, demonstrated an incredible level of human endurance and perseverance under duress.

Blaine's ordeal was not just a test of physical limits but also highlighted a critical aspect of the human spirit: the capacity to endure and persevere.

These qualities, while often interrelated, have distinct nuances. Patience often manifests in how we react to

---

1. 1. https://www.independent.co.uk/arts-entertainment/art/features/david-blaine-london-glass-box-stunt-reaction-starvation-above-the-below-a8523606.html

adversity, while endurance involves persisting despite obstacles. Consider the stories of actors or athletes who overcame poverty and violence to achieve success. They didn't allow their circumstances to define them but instead chose to push forward, embodying the essence of perseverance.

Both endurance and perseverance require a significant degree of self-control. For instance, throughout my career in the creative industry, I noticed a pattern within myself of leaving jobs every couple of years, indicating a lack of endurance on my part. It wasn't until I faced the challenges of trail running and an Ultra Marathon that I truly understood the value of perseverance. Trail running is something I enjoy partly because it is outdoors, but also because I love the unknown challenges the elements present. So when I signed up to do an Ultra Marathon in the Blue Mountains, endurance and perseverance were two words hammering away at me on every rocky incline, twist and turn. Although the word *ultra is* synonymous with the sport it also fittingly means to go beyond what is ordinary, proper, or moderate.[2] You pack a bag which contains all your nutrients, navigation equipment and protective gear. In the moments where my quad would lock up in pain and my IBT injury would rear its ugly head I had to find ways to push through the pain. Often I

---

2. https://www.merriam-webster.com/dictionary/ultra

thought about quitting, but I was in the middle of the mountains so either way I had to get back. Perseverance meant thinking of things I could do to make each step easier — listening to music, counting markers ahead of me, looking at my feet not the steep incline ahead of me. I'd also stop every 3km, I'd run, walk, run, walk. I broke every stretch of the route down into little chunks of victories. Different tricks or motivations to keep me going. Perseverance offered me the ability to act. Some would agree that endurance isn't a choice, perseverance is. But I could've equally made the choice to opt out of the race. In the moment endurance meant the ability to focus on *what is*. To make it to across the finish line I had to complete fifty kilometres. Perseverance is focusing on *what you can do* in spite of difficulty or lack of success, like what are the mechanics of survival I might tap into during the race. And this is where patience rises and where character is determined. Again, I'd argue patience and perseverance aren't mutually exclusive. Patience might require me to tolerate pain while perseverance seeks to find a way through the pain — a duality between *active* and *passive* patience. In the context of the Ultra when I felt like giving up I would stop, regather my thoughts and commit to little victories along the way to keep me going. Perseverance wouldn't have been possible without an element of patience and endurance was only possible once I managed to push through and make it to the end. To endure is the reality of completion. Had Blaine given up he might have persevered to a point, but he wouldn't have endured one of the greatest magic stunts to date. The opposing forces required an element of patience for him to find a way to overcome them. The analogy of a race, as cliched as it is, allows me to illustrate a very linear approach to how patience, endurance and perseverance interlink. I see it almost like this:

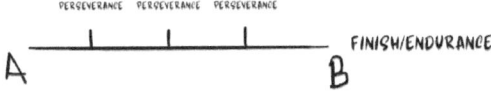

If you're wondering why I've omitted patience from my brilliant sketch above, it's because it's the manner in which one deals with delay i.e getting from point A to B. Patience is often subtle and harder to see in a race opposed to endurance or perseverance. Success is the result of having endured moments of setbacks through perseverance. Failure can very often be a precursor to success for those who aren't afraid to try and try again. Think of historical figures like Van Gogh, Henry Ford, and Thomas Edison to name a few, all of whom pushed on in spite of reaching early success. Some only realising it posthumously, like Van Gough. Having only ever sold one painting to a friend in his lifetime, he continued to paint a further eight hundred pieces. Whereas it took Edison a thousand different ways before creating a functional light bulb. Bankrupt and penniless, Ford failed five ventures before finding the successful motoring company. All life stories of endurance and perseverance along the way, yet, arguably, requiring the patience to keep on keeping on.

As I reflect on these personal experiences and the lessons learned from enduring challenges and persevering against odds, I find a profound connection with the timeless narratives in the Bible. Here, the concepts of endurance and patience are not just virtues but powerful tools for spiritual growth and resilience. The stories of King David and Moses, in particular, bring to life the essence of these qualities, as seen through the lens of faith, hope, and love. More importantly they offer profound insights into the relationship between endurance and patience. N.T. Wright, in his commentary on Colossians, delineates the subtle differences between the two:

> "God is accomplishing this productive and growing Christian character in his people so that they are strengthened with all power according to his glorious might. God is regularly seen in the Old Testament as the powerful God - the sovereign creator who rescued Israel

from Egypt. That power, unleashed through the gospel as now continually at work in God's people to given them great endurance and patience. Paul singles out these qualities as the weapons one needs to live in the world undaunted by its crises and panics. A patient and long-suffering spirit, the quiet corollary of faith, hope and love, is the product of the settled conviction that the Father of Jesus Christ is the sovereign Lord of the world, and that he is able to bring about his purposes in his own time and manner. There is a slight distinction to be drawn between 'endurance' and 'patience'. The former is what faith, hope and love bring to an apparently impossible situation, the latter what they show to an apparently impossible person."[3]

King David, for example, exemplified endurance through his faith and hope in God during his time hiding in caves from King Saul. Despite numerous opportunities for retribution, David chose faith, hope, and love, demonstrating patience even in dire circumstances. His heart and mind of good nature, instead giving praise throughout. We know this from reading various Psalms of David crying out and giving thanks to the Lord in the confines of the cave of Addulam — enough to force anyone in introspection and intercession. As Charles Spurgeon so rightly observes,

---

3. Wright, N. T. (1986). The Epistles of Paul to the Colossians and to Philemon : an introduction and commentary. United Kingdom: Inter-Varsity Press, 59-60.

"Caves make good closets for prayer; their gloom and solitude are helpful to the exercise of devotion. Had David prayed as much in his palace as he did in his cave, he might never have fallen into the act which brought such misery upon his later days."[4]

Clearly at his lowest, his faith pointed to a light at the end of the proverbial tunnel. So David does the only thing he can do and and falls back onto God by beginning the Psalm with a cry, but closing it in a song of praise. His frame of reference is not limited to the cave. Instead he rests on his rock and redeemer. His sight firmly fixed on what God can do and on what He will do, "You will deal bountifully with me" (Psalm 149:7 ESV). His endurance is what faith, hope and love bring to his "impossible situation": His love for God, his faith despite his difficult circumstances and his hope of walking free.

Similarly, Moses endured leading the Israelites through the wilderness, often facing ingratitude and rebellion. Yet, he displayed immense patience and grace, continually praying for his people and remaining steadfast in God's plan. Even till the bitter end of his days, he continued to lovingly lead the wayward Israelites. And of course, hoping they would eventually reach the promised

---

4. Spurgeon, Charles Haddon. The Treasury of David: Containing an Original Exposition of the Book of Psalms; a Collection of Illustrative Extracts from the Whole Range of Literature; a Series of Homiletical Hints Upon Almost Every Verse; and Lists of Writers Upon Each Psalm. United States: Funk & Wagnalls Company, 1886, 293.

Resilient Living: Endurance and Perseverance in Practice 53

land. This evidence of endurance, to reemphasise Wright's analogy is what *faith, hope and love bring to an apparently impossible situation*. Moses displayed great patience to an impossible people. Endurance to the the Israelites is what *faith, hope and love bring to an apparently impossible person(s)*.[5] Patience was a common theme throughout Moses's life, not just for him, but for the Israelites and most importantly not to forget God's own display of patience and His grace underpinning all.

These biblical narratives show that endurance and patience are not just virtues but essential tools for navigating life's challenges. They are the manifestation of faith, hope, and love in action. Our ultimate hope is in Christ's return and in the subsequent renewal and restoration of all creation. This is our understanding of the phrase, 'the Lord's coming' as we continue to endure and wait patiently for that day. Again, with Jesus we can experience fullness of life, the guarantee of the eternal trinity of values: faith, hope and love in overcoming the seemingly insurmountable. When Paul used these three words to encourage and spur the christian Thessalonians (1 Thessalonians 1:2-3) he structured it in a way that emphasised Jesus as the object of faith, hope, and love instead of merely the promises. What Paul means is our faith is in Christ, and our love is because of *Him* and directed to

---

5. Wright, N. T. (1986). The Epistles of Paul to the Colossians and to Philemon : an introduction and commentary. United Kingdom: Inter-Varsity Pres

Him and we persevere in hope towards *Him*. These exercise the spiritual qualities and reap what Christ intended because of the object of *Him*. Faith in itself requires action and perseverance in Him (Matthew 25:14-30). Love always hopes and perseveres (1 Corinthians 13:7 NIV). And we can have enduring hope, not because of what he has done in the New Testament but in the promises that are still to come (Hebrews 6:11).

The interplay of patience, endurance, and perseverance, underpinned by faith, hope, and love, forms the core of a resilient spirit. These qualities enable us to navigate life's trials and tribulations, constantly reminding us of God's sovereignty and the ultimate hope we have in Christ. Through patience and perseverance, we can endure life's challenges and emerge stronger, giving glory to God in all circumstances.

Losing your Patience

Impatience for victory guarantees defeat.

— Louis XIV

I spent Monday nights as a kid staying up late watching Seinfeld. Although I didn't get all the humour, I still found it absurdly comical. It was unlike any other show at the time. It didn't have the perfectly manicured moustache of Tom Selleck, the muscles of MR T, or the good-natured lessons learned in Full House. It was a show about nothing, yet something. Mostly idiosyncrasies. When I think about Seinfeld, it represents times when we mostly react when we shouldn't or wish we had said how we felt but didn't. In one particular episode called "The Nap". Jerry decided to get a kitchen makeover. The handyman he hired seemed nice enough but was excessively accommodating and kept interrupting Jerry over every little choice asking for his preference. "Do you want these hinges or these?" Irritated with his constant questions, Jerry eventually leaves his apartment, only to be interrupted again by the handyman who has one last important question to ask Jerry. Jerry has reached a boiling point of frustration and snaps back, saying that he doesn't care what the handyman chooses so long as the kitchen is finished by the time he gets back. He huffs and slams the door shut behind him. The script writes itself because when Jerry returns hours later, the handyman has installed an oversized, obtrusive design that Jerry shamefully accepts despite George, Elaine and Kramer's protest. The irony is that Jerry resorts to restoring the kitchen to its former state, only highlighting his indecisiveness and impatience.

 Impatience is often seen simply as a lack of patience. Yet, it's a complex vice, spurred by the conveniences of modern life, leading us to react impulsively. Admittedly we've all struggled with impatience, responding in ill-advised, illogical, impetuous ways. It's a wily vice which has wormed its way into modern life through the numerous conveniences we've come to expect. We can't bear the presence of falling into a slow-moving line, the time it takes for a kettle to boil, removing it seconds before the sound of a click and or waiting politely for someone to finish a sentence without interrupting them. Thinking about this causes my amygdala to rattle like a bullfrog trapped in a bucket. All signs, we would agree, of lacking patience. And, simply acknowledging that impatience is the antithesis of patience does a disservice in getting to the core of it as a behaviour. We can all agree there's an inherent Jerry trapped inside us that snaps when irritable. This reaction is a behavioural response of a particular mental and physical process triggered under direct circumstances, provoking characteristic types of definitive action. This trigger is in most cases always the result of having a goal in mind. It's whatever that point B is and ultimately realising that it's going to cost you more than you thought to reach it. In Jerry's case it was calling the handyman back to restore his kitchen to it's iconic former glory. If we were to flip the logic of comparing patience to impatience, it isn't a triggered response of equal measures. Yet, it is truer in definition and simplicity of lacking in patience than the former comparison. A patient person cannot simply be triggered to an impatient response where someone who lacks patience might have been. Equally a patient person doesn't render the virtue as a tool to overcome impatience. Either you are patient by virtue or lacking in response.

Today, our world offers ample opportunities for impatience. The evolution of technology and social interactions has complicated our lives, fragmenting them into a myriad of impatient moments. Reflecting on my childhood, communication was bound by time and cost. I could only speak to my friends on our landline telephone at a certain time of day that wasn't during peak hour costs. If I spoke too long I'd hear a thud on the wall from my dad reminding me to wrap up the conversation. This contrasts sharply with today's instant messaging culture. With the rise of technological progress so too are our lives confined to increasingly byzantine procedures. This shift has set a new norm for immediacy, as highlighted by a New York Times article on web users' intolerance for slow-loading pages.[1] It looked at the waiting time vs the speed at which websites are serving information. In 2009, a study by Forrester Research found that online shoppers expected pages to load in two seconds or fewer — and at three seconds, a large share abandoned the site. Only three years earlier a similar Forrester study found the average expectations for page load times were four seconds or fewer. And according to Google engineers, 400 milliseconds — literally the blink of an eye — is far too long to wait for information to load. The more the wheel of progress keeps turning and feeding rewards in minimal amount of wait times the more our expectations increase and become accustomed. When I think back to when I was a child, it was perfectly normal to go to your local library and search

---

1. A version of this article appears in print on March 1, 2012, Section A, Page 1 of the New York edition with the headline: For Impatient Web Users, an Eye Blink Is Just Too Long to Wait.

https://www.nytimes.com/2012/03/01/technology/impatient-web-users-flee-slow-loading-sites.html?smid=url-share numerous volumes of books for your assignment. Tirelessly flicking through Encyclopaedia Britannica's and photocopying pages, then cutting sections out and sticking them to a lined school book, colouring around the images with highlighters and writing in-between filling the pages with themes on the French Revolution or the life a bee. By the time I was in University I could search, download and paste in a matter of minutes, if not seconds.

The spectrum between wait times and receiving has decreased and the immediate shift between patience and impatience has increased. Technology today isn't slowing down. The more complicated it gets, the more knotty and entangled various part of lives become with one another. To a point where it becomes impossible to unravel, increasing our frustration and bringing with it unexpected costs. Costs that inevitably lead to anger and frustration.

I often wonder if impatience is cultivated the same way as one's personality or belief, an ongoing pattern or a more entrenched dynamic that's become instinctual — a social construct, dependent on historical and situational context, moulded over time. Impatience is this timeline in ones mind others might not share. It isn't an emotion in itself, but it does conjure underlying emotions due to it. These timelines echo our understanding of the world: our relationship with time, perspective, and how we think and act in our social settings. I know a significant reason I struggle with impatience is that it was part of my home life growing up. For all my father's many virtues, patience was not one of them. He would often soften this vice by substituting our surname. "Andersons don't wait. "I'm not impatient; I'm an Anderson". Although the most loving and compassionate man, he would blow his lid if he waited in the car for you longer than five minutes. My recollection of Sunday mornings doesn't spring to mind joyous car journeys heading to church, but of Dad honking at my mother to hurry up, followed by moaning and huffing for most of the way there. It felt like we were transporting another passenger of frustration. In the end, my father's anger at having to wait cost more than he realised, and he missed the opportunity to connect as a family, excited and filled with the joy of gathering. Years later, I understood where this residual annoyance manifested. My dad grew up in a regimental household. My grandfather was a fire inspector who ruled his house with fear and the precision timing of a train conductor's pocket watch. I remember peering through the crack of his bedroom door as he took off his prosthetic leg he so desperately tried to hide, along with the story of having lost it in the war fighting in North Africa. As he lifted his pink stump onto the bed, I could read grief on his face. Emotions were never spoken, and rules were drummed in with an iron fist. Punctuality was one of them. Dinner time was at 5:00 pm and not a minute later. And, so my father's repetition of never being late for an appointment was drummed into my brothers and I at a very early age. Generations of clock-watching and tapping feet. It's something I've carried through into my marriage. My wife was an hour and a half late for our first date. So, you can imagine how that played out in my mind. So, like my father and his father and probably his father, I would lose my patience when my wife was late for appointments. It got so bad that I would exaggerate departure time as a buffer to avoid any unsuspecting delays on the way or in the airport. In hindsight, I could see how my integrity of punctuality was blurred by short-tempered paranoia. While essential, the behavioural response to being on time should always advocate perspective and context. Sitting in traffic fuming at the vehicle travelling at a snail's pace in front of you won't get you where you're going any quicker. Nor will revving your car's engine incessantly at a red light in the hope that the roaring sound might prompt a change to green. It only highlights society's partiality to the reactionary behaviour of experiences learned and triggered.

Impatience isn't always detrimental. At times, it motivates us to pursue our goals with urgency. However, when impatience stems from a lack of faith, it becomes problematic. It challenges the trust in God's timing, as seen in the biblical stories of Abraham and Sarah, and King Saul. These narratives illustrate the negative consequences of impatience and the importance of trusting in God's plan.

On the other side of the spectrum one could argue patience isn't always necessarily a virtue. There are times when it hinders you, holding you back from seizing a moment. There might even be instances in our lives where doing things a little faster equals time and energy well spent. Is waiting always beneficial to getting what we want? And does getting something sooner close the gap of wasted time? I would argue impatience in and of itself is only good when it spurs us to realise what it takes to reach a goal or to deviate to a better one, or to maximise time not extend it. But I would equally argue that perhaps impatience is the wrong word to use. It is an emotional part of our repertoire which usually costs us for the wrong reasons whereas not exercising patience and instead being driven, determined, ambitious are positive adjectives that inevitably leads to positive outcomes. Impatience never has good motives at heart that are beneficial and positive beyond the self. It's not just a reactionary behaviour of personality, but it's lack of faith and trust in God. Nobody likes a backseat driver, especially God. Either you let him do the driving and trust He is going to get you where you're going or lean forward and take the steering wheel and see how it pans out. Impatience ultimately is a proud heart protesting God's timings on judgement and guidance. As Christians we are called to live by faith, to literally walk through life in trust and perseverance. Anything outside of that is a wayward path and separation from God. If impatience is void of love, then there's is no place for God and all hope and trust in Him is lost and replaced with doubt of His wisdom.

When impatience stems from a lack of faith, it becomes problematic. It challenges the trust in God's timing, as seen in the biblical story of Abraham and Sarah. Right from the start God was clear in His promise in which their descendants will be as *numerous as the stars* (Genesis 15:1-6). For Sarah, or any woman for that matter, it's understandable doubt would set in. The worry of being too old to bear children would be at the forefront of anyone's mind and be good reason to trigger an emotional response from impatience. Unbelief was deeply at the core otherwise Sarah's advice for Abraham to take Sarah's handmaid Hagar to have a child would not have bore Ishmael. Yet in spite of God's continual and reassuring promise over the years they still chose to not remain patient (Genesis 16). Many years later at the ripe old age of one hundred for Moses and ninety-nine for Sarah did God's promise eventually comes true. Isaac was the child of promise not Ishmael. What transpired was years of conflict and division due to both lineages. Without getting too deep in the weeds of historical theology and politics there remains today various schools of thought concerning the two decedents of Isaac (Jews) and Ishmael (Arabs) that perpetuate the division of Israel and Palestine hindering any further reconciliation. One thing we can be certain of is the division amongst Ishmael and Isaac was purely because the inheritance was given to the latter. This story isn't about anger or family division, but instead a manifestation of unbelief towards God's wisdom and timing. Impatience is at the heart of the narrative continually challenging God's promise. We see this time and time again throughout the bible of humanities proud and arrogant heart unsatisfied with God's timing, unwilling to wait to and trust in His timing. It's a reminder for us when we think inaction is weakness and choose to take matters into our own hands it inevitably will always come at a cost. The cost of Abraham and Sarah refusing to wait and impatiently seeking what their heart so desired resulted in decades of generational conflict.

My career path reflects my struggles with impatience, leading me to make hasty decisions in pursuit of immediate satisfaction. My resume looks like a hopscotch board having jumped ship at jobs often for reasons that felt sparkly and new, lured by money, benefits and an anthemic company manifesto only to be disappointed and disheartened months later. This impulsive approach, driven by a misguided search for happiness, overlooked the value of patience and trust in God's guidance. Patience and impatience serve as reminders to evaluate our lives' priorities. The apostle Paul's words from prison encapsulate this sentiment, emphasising the value of knowing Christ above all earthly pursuits:

> But whatever were gains to me I now consider loss for the sake of Christ. What is more, I consider everything a loss because of the surpassing worth of knowing Christ Jesus my Lord, for whose sake I have lost all things. I consider

them garbage, that I may gain Christ (Philippians 3:7-8 NIV).

Impatience often comes as a result of not surrendering to a situation that we really cannot fight.

In the tapestry of life, the threads of patience and impatience are interwoven, each adding its hue to the fabric of our existence. Our journey through time is marked by moments when patience illuminates the path with grace, and instances when impatience propels us forward, for better or worse. Yet, at the heart of this intricate weave lies a profound truth: the moments we choose patience over impatience are not merely pauses in the rush of life but opportunities to align our will with the divine. As we stand at the crossroads of decision, may we find the wisdom to discern when to wait and when to act, understanding that in the grand design of the Creator, every moment of patience is a step towards a fuller, deeper trust in the unfolding plan of a world beyond our immediate sight. In embracing patience, we open ourselves to the possibility of a life enriched not by the fleeting victories of haste, but by the enduring peace of a soul in harmony with the eternal rhythm of creation.

Part Two
Cultivating Patience

The Practice of Patience

> The key to everything is patience. You get the chicken by hatching the egg, not by smashing it.
>
> — Arnold H. Glasow

A METAFICTIONAL MAGNUM OPUS SITS ON MY SHELF, unread. Admittedly, each glance at it evokes an imaginary cackle, mocking me as a reader unfulfilled. It reminds me of my futile existence and the irony of its title: *Infinite Jest*.[1] Whether you love or loathe him, I know more about David Foster Wallace, having never read a single book of his. One Sunday morning, amid a weekend of torrential

---

1. Wallace, David Foster. *Infinite Jest*. Little, Brown and Company, 1996.

showers, I mindlessly scrolled through YouTube when I stumbled upon a commencement speech, 'DFW', delivered to a graduating class at Kenyon College, Ohio.[2] The entire transcript is available in a book titled *This Is Water*.[3] He begins with a parable-like story of two young fish swimming along. An older fish, swimming in the opposite direction, passes by them and says, "Morning boys, how's the water?" The fish smile in response and continue on their way. Later, one fish turns to the other and asks, "What the hell is water?" DFW's point is profound: like the fish unaware they are swimming in water, "the most obvious, ubiquitous, important realities are often the ones hardest to see and talk about". He elaborates, "Learning how to think means learning to exercise some control over how and what you think. It means being conscious and aware enough to choose what you pay attention to and how you construct meaning from experience". The art of thinking derives from the conscious decision to engage with our surroundings thoughtfully, even in the most mundane moments.

Life, in its essence, is the practice of patience — not only employing it in our daily lives but also consciously applying it. Our default setting, unchecked, often opposes life's many virtues, gravitating towards greed, selfishness,

---

2. Best English Speeches: David Foster Wallace "This is Water." (with BIG Subtitles) https://www.youtube.com/watch?v=ms2BvRbjOYo
3. Wallace, David Foster. This Is Water: Some Thoughts, Delivered on a Significant Occasion, about Living a Compassionate Life. United States: Little, Brown, 2009.

and impatience. Recently, while waiting in a long checkout line at the supermarket, my frustration was palpable—I was the embodiment of impatience, visibly aggrieved by the presence of only two cashiers. My behaviour, far from hastening the process, merely showcased my petulance. Had I been more attuned to my thoughts, I might have considered the many reasons for the delay: a possible staff shortage due to an ill cashier or perhaps budget cuts leading to understaffing. The woman ahead, seemingly slowing the queue, might have been preparing for a significant celebration or coping with a recent loss. This scenario illustrates that a shift in mindset, from a default reaction to a chosen response, can vastly alter our perception. As David J. Lieberman suggests in *Never Get Angry Again*,

> "Perspective lies at the crux of our response and explains why we often feel irritated in the heat of the moment. After a few minutes, our anger subsides. A few hours later, we feel less angry, and in a few days, we wonder why we got so bothered in the first place. Time provides perspective, allowing us to see the situation with clarity. Likewise, as we grow and mature, we look back on our lives and realise that the summer camps we thought we *must* attend, the person we thought we *must* be friends with, or the office job we thought we *must* be offered are

no longer *musts*. Without perspective, we are forever like a lost child with a broken toy."[4]

Patience is a virtue that doesn't come effortlessly; it requires deliberate practice and awareness, especially in how we respond to our circumstances. The concept of 'surrendering' in psychological terms often means countering the impulse to control every aspect of our lives. Despite its connotations of passivity, surrender is not about defeat but humility. In Christianity, surrendering to God is not out of fear but awe (Y*irah* in Hebrew). It's a gesture of respect, acknowledging our limitations before our Creator. "We deny ourselves and take up our cross to follow Him" (Matthew 16:24), embodying a profound form of patience that transcends mere waiting.

During a 4X4 road trip through Namibia with my friend Dave, before he embraced Christianity, we delved into deep conversations about faith. Amidst the backdrop of the Namib desert, a discussion emerged about surrendering to God.

"There's part of me that wants to believe, I do"

"So what's stopping you?" I replied.

---

[4]. Lieberman, Dr. David J.. Never Get Angry Again: The Foolproof Way to Stay Calm and in Control in Any Conversation Or Situation. United States: St. Martin's Publishing Group, 2018.Loc 37

"It's the idea of being submissive, that I have to somehow surrender to *this* God".

"But why do you see it as a negative thing?" I asked.

"This notion that I need to be on bended knee and submissively surrendering goes against everything in my character". He paused and looked out the window at the dusty road and the sand caking the window building up residue on the corners. "I don't want to be this weak, pathetic soul, everything in my body wants to take control and be the master of my own destiny instead of sitting back and expecting something miraculous to happen."

I gripped firmly on the steering wheel and passionately went on an excitable rant.

"Dave, quite the contrary, it's nothing more than a social misconception. I can totally understand why you view it in that way, most people see this sky god who is an unapproachable deity living somewhere up there, I point to sunroof where the midday sun is beating down through the sand caked window. "He doesn't live there, he's inside here Dave".

I sweep my hand across my chest, placing my palm on the right side over my heart.

"A relationship with God isn't like a headmaster and pupil parallel, you don't need to fear being scolded for not having your shirt tucked in. All you have to do Dave is let go. There's power and freedom in not always trying to live for ourselves, in fact there is strength in doing so. It's easy for you to reach over and take the wheel. We all get an urge to want to steer our own course, but we also sometimes get tired, or lost, and we take a wrong turn, and in those moments it isn't foolish to pull to the side of the road and switch seats is it? Just as you and I have been doing this whole trip after a couple of hours. Does that make me weak, or humble enough to understand the fact I can't do this road alone if I want to get to where I'm needed to go?"

I paused for a bit to wet my lips from the humid heat.

"It's also okay to not always have the answers."

"I know, but when you have been taught your whole life that you are responsible for your life and the choices you make, it's hard to suddenly let go of that", he responded.

"There is more in life that we are powerless over than what we actually can control", I said, "You're not weak for surrendering Dave, you're strong — it's how you choose to see that."

Dave's resistance stemmed from a reluctance to submit, equating it with weakness. However, surrendering, or letting go, is not a sign of weakness but a testament to strength — the strength to acknowledge our human limitations and embrace a power greater than ourselves. This reframe — viewing surrender not as defeat but as liberation — offers a new perspective on patience and faith.

Patience, therefore, is not a passive waiting but an active engagement with life, guided by a conscious choice to think differently. It's about reframing our thoughts, stepping away from our ego, and allowing ourselves to be led by a higher purpose. Such patience is cultivated through daily practices: mindfulness, gratitude, empathy, and sometimes, simply allowing ourselves to wait. The journey of patience is rooted in the way we choose to see the world and respond to it, understanding that often, we control far less than we think but can still find strength in surrendering.

Our journey through life, with its trials and tribulations, is a testament to the patience bestowed upon us and the patience we must cultivate. As the Bible illustrates, patience is a divine attribute; it's a calling to endure, to remain steadfast in faith amidst life's challenges, and to always focus on the higher purpose set before us.

Part of thinking differently in situations is learning to trust and living in accord with the Holy Spirit to help direct and guide us to practice patience no matter what situation we are faced with. Paul talks of this in Galatians,

> "But the Holy Spirit produces this kind of fruit in our lives: love, joy, peace, patience, kindness, goodness, faithfulness, gentleness, and self-control. There is no law against these things!" (Galatians 5:22-23 NLT).

Learning to yield to the Spirit will help us grow, but also reshape our capacity and response to patience. Patience has a lot to do with where we place our thinking, where we put or trust, direct our thankfulness and what we allow our thoughts to gravitate towards. If our thoughts are on what is right in front of us, or we choose to latch on to something negative, it only makes sense that our response is manifested from within outwards. So if I choose to feel irritated inside because my wife has said something to me which perhaps I didn't want to hear, my natural inclination is to snap back at her without much thought. If I allow my mind to be ruled by my immediate emotions, my focus is *reactionary* not *Christ-like*. Although impatience from my response is an outward act, it is inherently rooted in selfishness and pride. As the wisdom book, Ecclesiastes, tells us,

> "...and the patient in spirit is better than the proud in spirit" (Ecclesiastes 7:8 NKJV).

And, the apostle Paul calls us to,

> "...set our minds on thing above, not on things on earth" (Colossians 3:2 NKJV).

If we keep our mind on walking in the spirit, focussed on above and not towards life's consternations, we'll be able to be patient *with all* (1 Thessalonians 5:14). Walking in God's will is essential to the Christian disposition, not only to practice the gift of patience, but to live a moral, godly life sustained by the gifts of the Holy Spirit. The fruit of the Spirit are perfections that are formed in us as first fruit of eternal glory.

. . .

The scriptures remind us of the virtue of patience, not just as a means to endure but as a way to live fully, guided by faith and trust in something greater than ourselves. Patience is more than just a virtue to aspire to; it's a practice that shapes our very being, our interactions, and our outlook on life. It's a journey of growth, learning, and ultimately, understanding the profound truth that the essence of life, much like the water to the fish, is often right before our eyes, waiting to be acknowledged and embraced. Every moment, slice of life and challenge is an opportunity to put it into practice. And it starts by consciously doing two things: firstly reframing your thought patterns to not only look at the self as life isn't only about you. You are part of a much bigger story with many other characters also living out their own. Secondly, turn away from the self and let the spirit of God lead you — this is what it means to deny our flesh. Flesh is inward focus, to deny it means to focus outward. The Holy Spirit has no experience with anything opposite to love. That's the language of our flesh. Instead turn your eyes, heart and mind outwards and think of Christ who suffered such hostility against himself by those who were too blind to see and impatient to hear, that you may not grow weary in your soul and give up (2 Corinthians 3:17-18 NET).

The Beauty in Stillness

No great thing is created suddenly.

— Epictetus

I LOVE ART GALLERIES. HOWEVER, I DON'T ADORE them in the way my wife does. My approach is to conquer them at a breathless pace, much like scrolling through an Instagram feed. On the other hand, she stops intermittently at every piece, approaching each artwork with hermeneutical enthusiasm. While enjoyable for my wife, it's painstakingly infuriating for me. The entire experience feels akin to someone telling a long, drawn-out story when you only want them to get to the point. My university studies of Susan Sontag's book *Against interpretation* largely influenced my rapid-gallery walkthrough.[1] The core of her argument is her opposition to contemporary, formalist interpretation, where observers place excessive importance and interpretation upon the meaning of a piece of art. Instead, she advocates for a focus on the sensuous aspects of a work: how it appears and whatever it invokes. What do you feel? Does it move you? Perhaps taking her belief that "interpretation is the revenge of the intellect upon art" too seriously, I decided that if a painting or photograph didn't immediately evoke an emotion in me, it was time to move on. And move on I did, cycling through emotions: happy, sad, troubled, indifferent, Next! I'm not alone in my hasty approach to cultural excursions.

According to a study published in the Journal of Empirical Studies of the Arts, visitors to The Metropolitan Museum of Art in New York were observed as they browsed the museum's collection and discovered that, on average, most visitors spend just seventeen seconds looking at an individual artwork.[2] This propensity explains my impatient zipping through museums like the Louvre or Musée d'Orsay, barely pausing to appreciate the art. Even the Sagrada Familia became more of a brisk morning walk than a leisurely appreciation of architectural marvels. Despite this, in my mind, each experience

---

1. Sontag, Susan. Against Interpretation and Other Essays. United Kingdom: Penguin Books Limited, 2013.
2. Smith, Jeffrey K., and Lisa F. Smith. "Spending Time on Art." Empirical Studies of the Arts 19, no. 2 (July 2001): 229–36. https://doi.org/10.2190/5MQM-59JH-X21R-JN5J.

remains memorable, whether absorbed in minutes or hours. My wife contends that I lack the patience to truly let the art speak to me on a deeper level, beyond immediate emotions, to hear and see what it's saying. I disagree.

To her defence, Professor Jennifer L. Roberts in an article published in the Harvard Review, posits that the only way to 'release the richness' held by a painting is by observing it for the time it demands, until it physically impacts us. She demonstrates this with her students by assigning them to observe a single work of art for three hours. This exercise is not merely about looking but about seeing. "Just because something is available instantly to vision does not mean that it is available instantly to consciousness. Or, in slightly more general terms: access is not synonymous with learning. What turns access into learning is time and strategic patience." [3]

Roberts highlights the urgency of modelling awareness of time and patience as productive mediums of learning, especially in our fast-paced world. She argues that "a deliberate engagement of delay no longer connotes disempowerment but instead invokes power." Intrigued, I decided to test this notion and give art the time of day, even if it meant standing before a piece all day. So I put this to practice one Saturday morning. With my daughter in tow, I visited an exhibition by the 18th-century Australian

---

3. Roberts, Jennifer L. The Power of Patience: Teaching students the value of deceleration and immersive attention. November — 2013. www.harvardmagazine.com/sites/default/files/pdf/2013/11-pdfs/1113-40.pdf

impressionist, Arthur Streeton. His landscapes initially struck me as repetitive — once you've seen one, you've seen them all, I thought. Yet, I pressed on at a deliberately slower pace. Eventually, I paused at a painting that didn't stand out in his collection but felt different because of the subject's angle. My eyes were drawn down through a gorge, flanked by cliffs at sixty-degree angles, framing a field of sugar plains below—a tapestry of short, thick coloured strokes. The natural light's play on the gorge, set against the shadowed valley below, was mesmerising. It was as if the painting invited me in, nudging me to take flight, with my daughter's pram handle becoming a makeshift hang glider. The moment of imagined flight was interrupted by my daughter's cry for apple juice, echoing us to move on.

Reflecting on this experience, I realised that stopping to observe art requires a conscious effort but also opens up space for imagination and interpretation to flourish. Now, whenever I see that painting, I remember the feeling it evoked. My little experiment embodied what Professor Roberts intended for her students: to encourage a slow-down, allowing patience to reveal itself as a skill.

"It's a very old idea that patience leads to skill, of course — but it seems urgent now to consider patience itself as the skill to be learned," Roberts notes.[4]

This idea is also celebrated globally through a cultural

---

4. Bailey, Anna. Slow art? It will 'blow your mind'. 5 April 2019. www.bbc.com/news/entertainment-arts-47699001

initiative, Slow Art Day, an event that aims to train the eye to observe by slowing down and letting the art speak.

Every external pressure — social and technological — pushes us towards immediacy and away from the mysteries unveiled through patience. In Japan, a resurgence of interest in traditional arts and crafts among the younger generation serves as a counterpoint to our technologically driven age. The art of Kogei, or engineered art, emphasises the importance of traditional techniques and materials, underscoring patience and mastery. According to the Japanese Ministry of Education, Science, and Culture, in order for an object to be recognised as a traditional Japanese ancient craft it must meet all five requirements:

1. The item must be practical enough for regular use.
2. The item must predominantly be handmade.
3. The item must be crafted using traditional techniques.
4. The item must be crafted using traditional materials.
5. The item must be crafted at its place of origin.[5]

---

[5]. Goto, K. (2019). Crafts Policies in Japan. In: Mignosa, A., Kotipalli,

One such art dates back to before 5000 BCE and involves holding a *natsume* — a small, round container used for matcha (green tea powder) during tea ceremonies — in one hand. In the other a *funzutsu* — a hollow quill from a crane feather, the tip covered with silk. The trick, or I should say the art, is to gently flick the tool sprinkling the gold filings precisely onto the timber surface of the *natsume*, shaping delicate moss that snakes off the branches of a pine tree. By no means is this easy, for some this specialised skill can take up to three years to master, but often up to five years to complete each of the painstakingly delicate craftwork. The resulting works sell to collectors and museums for tens of thousands. This is commonly known as the traditional Japanese craft of Urushi, often referred to as lacquerware (*Shikki*), not to be confused with the European derivative. The word *urushi* is said to come from two Japanese words — *uruosu*, which means *to moisten*, and *uruwashi* meaning *beautiful*. The sap of the Japanese varnish tree (Toxicodendron Vernicifluum) produces and oil and is carefully extracted. A single *urushi* tree produces only 150ml of sap each four-month harvesting season, after which it is cut down and takes another 15 years to grow. So not only is the craft time consuming, but so too is the cultivation. What's even equally interesting is this same sap is used by buddhist monks to preserve themselves in a form of self-mummifica-

---

P. (eds) A Cultural Economic Analysis of Craft. Palgrave Macmillan, Cham. https://doi.org/10.1007/978-3-030-02164-1_10

tion known as *sokushinbutsu* — entering the last stages while still alive. The monk drinks a tea made from the sap, which dehydrates the body and the toxins prevent any insect or bacterial infestation. In a strange, almost poetic connection this tree acts as a life form of preservation and as a slowing-down process in both cases.

Whether through observing art or mastering a craft, the practice of patience emerges as a crucial skill, revealing the depth and richness of experience often overlooked in our hurried lives. This profound relationship between time, effort, and outcome is a reminder that beauty and meaning are not things to be rushed. The slower, more intentional processes of creation — like those seen in Urushi and other traditional crafts — challenge the very pace at which we live today. They suggest that the rewards we seek, whether in art or in life, are not merely in the result but in the careful unfolding of the process itself. By valuing patience, we open ourselves to a more thoughtful existence, one that invites reflection, nurtures mastery, and allows for a deeper connection with the world around us.

Jesus, too, embodied the virtue of patience through a craft, honed through years of carpentry. His familiarity with wood and craftsmanship wasn't just a trade but a preparation for his ultimate purpose. His education began with the first grain of wood. For roughly eighteen years (over a decade), the son of a stonemason, Jesus chiseled, planed, sanded and knocked nails into wood. He became obsessively familiar with the same material and tools which, in a cruel irony would inevitably shape the ultimate masterpiece of God's plan. Little did He know, or maybe He did, this would become a formative eduction on his understanding of the virtue of patience. Firstly, the craft and trade of working with wood was often an exercise in patience , imagination and frustration. There's an old woodworking saying, measure twice, cut once. Haste is the enemy of perfection. But like any good carpenter Jesus would've spent his days studying the grain of wood, figuring the hardness, ascertaining where the knots were, finding the colour patterns and working the best way to cut it. Sawing perfectly in the same direction or cross grain. Anyone who's worked with wood knows how it tests your patience. Even the most skilled carpenter has fallen short with a wayward cut or measurement annoyingly off by millimetres. Jesus literally took up our human nature and learned the most basic skill of patience. I believe it's no coincidence He chose this occupation with purpose. He needed to ready his body by carrying timber and stone. The toughened hands of the carpenter exemplified his full humanity as Jesus patiently waited before embarking on his messianic ministry. While learning to slowly craft a finished product from wood, He himself was slowly being refined and shaped into his ultimate purpose. His life was all planning and preparation for His ultimate purpose. He waited on God's time to be revealed and in the process learned submission, obedience through everyday labour.

"Though He was a Son, *yet* He learned obedience by the things which He suffered. And having been perfected, He became the author of eternal salvation to all who obey Him" (Hebrews 5:9 NKJV). Almost as a full circle tragedy of his own life, the same hands that carried and hauled wood and hammered nails as a youngster would be the same hands that would painstakingly lug the heavy load of the cross on his back eventually having nails pounded into his weathered hands, while the onlookers waited and Jesus patiently hung finally waiting for God's timing once again and to be with Him forevermore. In the end, Jesus' journey — from carpenter to saviour— illustrates that patience, learned and practiced, shapes not only skill but character, leading us to fulfil our ultimate purpose.

Patience is not just a virtue but a necessary skill for depth and understanding. Whether through the deliberate observation of art, the painstaking creation of traditional crafts, or the life of Jesus as a carpenter albeit the ultimate sacrifice, patience allows us to uncover layers of meaning and experience often hidden by our rush for immediacy. By slowing down and embracing patience, we open ourselves to a richer, more fulfilling existence, where every moment holds the potential for profound discovery and growth. This practice of patience not only enhances our appreciation of the world around us but also shapes our character, guiding us toward our ultimate purpose with grace and insight.

How to Peel an Orange

In a world filled with distractions, the person who can maintain focus has an immense advantage.

— Unknown

I WILL NEVER FORGET MY DAUGHTER'S FIVE WORDS one Saturday morning: "Daddy, put down your phone and look at me." It felt like a punch to the gut. All she wanted was for me to be present, and she could not understand why a small screen I was holding seemed more important than her. It wasn't, and I could not tell you what I was looking at if I tried. It was unimportant, yet it had a firm hold on my attention over my daughter for some reason. This experience is nothing new or exclusive. The modern age is designed to win attention -- a time when information bombards us from every direction. There is something very Darwinian about it, except we are not the hunters but the hunted.

All of this hits closer to home for me, having worked for a popular social media platform. Every meeting, forecast, and strategy is built to win the market share of attention. Its whole existence and future rests on the success of eyeballs. I often talked to brands about how they could successfully create ads for diverse attention. A win for them was a win for the platform, as long as the time spent on the platform increased along with its users. Admittedly, I never liked the term "users," but a spade is a spade, and we have all spiralled into addictive habits. Of course, like all digital platforms, they sprouted an altruistic message of well-being and happiness — making the world a better place, connecting you to your loved ones, and creating a space to express yourself freely. This, however, is no different to Plato's cave — the allegory of the dancing shadows on the wall where he warns, "Those who can see beyond the shadows and lies of their culture will never be understood, let alone believed by the masses".[1] It has become the new normal through which we live our lives. The irony is that in this world of immediacy, there are apps designed to slow you down, clear your head, and even calm you. However, they share and live in a space

---

1. Plato. *The Republic*. Translated by G.M.A. Grube, revised by C.D.C. Reeve. Indianapolis: Hackett Publishing Company, 1992, 514a-520a.

that keeps you from this. This is not a rant about the digital revolution, but if we are to understand patience, we must understand where the shadows on the wall are coming from and step out of the proverbial cave.

Amid the irony of being distracted by my mobile phone, what began as a simple search for a specific recipe led me down YouTube's algorithm-driven rabbit hole, where I found myself watching a string of videos showcasing clever hacks for peeling an orange quickly and efficiently. I'm talking from scissors and knives to your own hands. While I recognise the challenge in peeling an orange, be it messy or time-consuming, I never imagined so many people on the internet shared their pursuit of the ultimate peeling technique. I did, however, come across an interesting story about a monastic monk living in a community with a specific daily practice. Every day, they would be given an orange with the simple task of quietly sitting somewhere for an hour and peeling it slowly. Unlike the YouTube influencers, the monks focused less on immediacy and more on latency. Their supposed hack was quite the opposite. As such, they would seek to find ways to effectively try to peel the skin of the orange in one motion without ever breaking it. The reward was eventually in the eating, but the point of the exercise was to put focus and patience into practice. Thomas à Kempis, the German-Dutch canon and author of the classic "The Imitation of Christ," said: "All men commend patience, although few are willing to practice it."[2] This is very much the ethos of the monks who remain still in the moment and are also learning the lesson of delayed gratification by savouring the orange before consumption. Smelling the top note of fragrance and feeling the thick, pitted, leathery rind of the orange skin with each peel. Eventually, tasting the tangy, luscious sparks of citrus euphoria.

Can you imagine how different halftime during a kiddy football match would be if everyone did what the monks did and stopped to slowly peeled their orange, savouring the moment, before eating? I certainly cannot fathom sitting somewhere for an hour and peeling an orange in such a way. I wonder what it would be like if everyone did this during their lunch break. What would returning to your desk feel like? How focused would people be and perhaps less stressed? We're so used to having food designed to quickly shove in our mouth with one hand while clutching a mouse or a mobile phone in the other. All for the ingenuity of multi-tasking. Yet, an orange forces you to stop. It cannot be peeled with one hand or consumed without wiping your hands and mouth. It is as if God created the orange to make it hard enough to peel, only to slow you down. The orange is the proverbial traffic light reminder to delay instant gratification and to slow down in the name of patience.

---

2. à Kempis, Thomas. *The Imitation of Christ*. Translated by William Creasy. Notre Dame, IN: Ave Maria Press, 1989, 39

I'm reminded of an analogy often used in time management principles. Dealing with large tasks, which feel elephant-sized, can usually leave you feeling overwhelmed. Commonly referred to as the elephant technique, this concept examines how to tackle eating an elephant. Most of us would attempt to bite off more than we could chew; however, the only way to eat it with our tiny human mouths is by making the elephant smaller. Some would distance themselves far enough for the elephant to appear scaled down, some would spend hours stretching their mouths, while others would divide the mammal into bite-size portions, making it more manageable to eat. In life, we are going to be faced with what often feels like insurmountable tasks and challenges. This is inevitable. The point is not to feel overwhelmed and impatient but to tackle it one bit at a time. Of course, there most likely will be techniques to make a task less time-consuming, but invariably, like the elephant analogy, it will require managing the sum of parts rather than the whole. Either way, time management is a result of careful planning and consideration. Time isn't a servant to your frustration or anger by feeling overwhelmed. It is a partner that works alongside you to achieve the required results. An athlete lives alongside time. Time spent in the gym, on the field during practice, and eating correctly. All this time invested means better field, track, or swimming pool results. Time isn't a servant or a master but a support alongside you, providing clarity and input. Time sidles up to the monks who peel the oranges to clear their heads from distractions and learn to be in the moment. To truly savour what's right before them, enjoying the proverbial fruits of their labour.

My friend Brian is an intelligent guy. He's always thinking up schemes and ideas in his head. He has the personality of an entrepreneur but lacks the drive. Ever since I've known him, he would rattle off harebrained ideas and projects in his head: "I want to write a book," "I have a great idea for a movie." "Hey, I'm considering quitting my job to start a charity." His close friends gave him the nickname ScatterBrian. When he would corner one of us with one of his new dreams or passions, we would refer to it as having been scatterBrianed. He had an impulsive knack for jumping from idea to idea in days without taking considered time to focus on one first. Every idea we thought was brilliant would never make it off the ground due to haste. He would start one project, and a month later, when asked how he was getting on, we were met with a response of excuses. "Too busy", or "I've had an even better idea," or "The world's against me", and so on. Although I always sensed his frustration, he would lift his spirits by equalising the failures with another new, exciting distraction or project on the horizon. I eventually grew frustrated with his impatience. He would look for every other way to tackle the proverbial elephant without actually tackling it one bit at a time. Instead of breaking his projects into achievable portions, he would move from one elephant to the next. A bite here, a chew there and on and on he would go. Empty-handed with an empty stomach. All I could see was a lot of unnecessary wasted elephants. How could he ever complain about opportunities without giving them any time? Eventually, it got to a point where I was bored with hearing the same tired ending. I, too, needed to practice my patience. So, my advice to him was loving but forthright. I told him I wanted to hear another idea when he focused enough to see it through. It's been eleven years since I told him that. He's now in his forties, married with children, and has yet to see his next "project" through. Most of the time, like with Brian, the battle is in the mind, but wisdom is taking the time and a step back to see things. Patience is a pre-setter to well-being. Patience offers clarity and, in turn, leads to less anxiety, stress, worry, fear and, most of all, procrastination. The well-being of the soul and mind requires the patience to consistently see something through, no matter the size of the elephant.

I, like most, tend to harbour several tasks in my head like a squirrel storing nuts. I jump between tasks instead of knocking them off one by one. Multitasking makes it even harder to manage an uninterrupted life. Frustration and impatience rear their ugly heads when little or no progress has been made. Cal, Newport, in his book Deep Work stresses the notion that the more you try to do, the less you accomplish, but rather approach it incrementally, "Three to four hours a day, five days a week, of uninterrupted and carefully directed concentration, it turns out, can produce a lot of valuable output."³ To wedge another Seinfeld analogy, Cal references a conversation between Jerry and another comic on a crucial life hack, "The way to be a better comic was to create better jokes," and then explains that creating better jokes was to write daily. Seinfeld continued by describing a specific technique he used to help maintain this discipline. He keeps a calendar on his wall. Every day he writes jokes, he crosses out the date on the calendar with a big red X. "After a few days, you'll have a chain," says Seinfeld. "Just keep at it, and the chain will grow longer daily. You'll like seeing that chain, especially when you get a few weeks under your belt. Your only job next is not to break the chain." This chain method (as some now call it) soon became a hit among writers and fitness enthusiasts — communities that thrive on the ability to do hard things consistently." Seinfeld has come out since refuting he came up with or even used this strategy. Either way, it makes a whole lot of sense. Keep taking small bites of the elephant.

It's apparent patience is a skill practised over time — and in doing so, it creates a space beneficial to your mental well-being. Patience isn't just a virtue but a positive state of mind. When I am stuck in traffic, it leaves me impatient

---

3. Newport, Cal. *Deep Work: Rules for Focused Success in a Distracted World*. Grand Central Publishing, 2016.

and enraged. I don't arrive home running through the doors, gliding across the wooden floor in a joyful state like Tom Cruise in the movie Cocktail. I sometimes open the door, furiously throw my keys and jacket down, and seek my poor wife like a keen-eyed fighter pilot only so I can moan at someone. "Honey, you won't believe it..." I rattle off. My mental state is already in a negative space, and by bringing that home with me, I'm treading on fertile ground for seeing new arguments arise. The notion of *Keep Calm and Carry On* becomes that I'm irritable and can't move on until I've vented. It's moving the needle of my mental state towards negative emotions and increasing the risk of anxiety and possibly depression. In a 2007 study, Professor Sarah A. Schnitker and Professor Robert A. Emmons concluded the positive effects patience had on the mind. "People who exhibit patience tend to show more gratitude, empathy and compassion towards humanity."[4] In 2012, Schnitker unpacked the attributes of patience for positive, healthy outcomes by identifying three key variants: interpersonal, life hardships, and daily hassles.[5] Interpersonal is the communication and relationships with those you deal with daily. It could be a friend, a colleague

---

4. Schnitker, S. A., & Emmons, R. A. (2007). Patience as a virtue: Religious and psychological perspectives. *Research in the Social Scientific Study of Religion, 18,* 177–207.
https://doi.org10.1163ej.9789004158511.i-301.69
5. Sarah A. Schnitker (2012): An examination of patience and well-being, The Journal of Positive Psychology: Dedicated to furthering research and promoting good practice, 7:4, 263-280
DOI: 10.1080/17439760.2012.697185

or a partner. And, within any of these interactions, it's the knack to navigate your way around angry, upset, and annoying people with aplomb. It's far easier for me to spar with my wife over dirty dishes instead of looking at the bigger picture (common sense) and applying patience to work as a team. With life hardships, it's the shift in mentality of seeing the glass half full when approaching frustrating setbacks. What is the silver lining to a father who's recently been made redundant — having the patience, something else (possibly better) will arrive? Patience to also make the most of the situation — a chance to spend more time with your family or start that project collecting dust in the garage. Thirdly, patience over daily hassles is the most common and frequent display. It could be suppressing your temper when the toilet's blocked, when the internet is down, or when your wife's prized cushions become a canvas to your two-year-old's magic marker masterpiece. When patience is deployed, all three of these instances surface positive responses. Interpersonal patience reveals hope and satisfaction, patience through life's hardships reveals courage and hope, and patience over daily hassles reveals satisfaction and optimism. The good thing is that it proves that patience pays off for those already exercising it in their everyday situations. The other thing is that it provides hope to apply this skill and become more patient over time.

As a Christian, my first response whenever I am digging deep in restraint and seeking patience is I naturally turn to God through prayer and supplication. "God, please grant me patience to get through this awkward meeting." "God, I'm trying to remain calm when my daughter refuses to listen; please give me patience." "God, give me patience while I watch The Bachelor with my wife."

The Bible is full of prayers for patience (which I cover later). We've all prayed for patience, but have you ever learned patience through prayer? Spending time in the Word requires a profound amount of discipline and patience. Meditating every morning on the gospel and praying is like peeling an orange for me. Sometimes, opening an orange would be easier than opening Leviticus.

Interestingly, researchers have studied the impact prayer has on mental health. A study led by Harvard Professor Tyler J. VanderWeele discovered that young people who regularly prayed showed fewer signs of depression but greater self-esteem and were more satisfied in life than those who never prayed at all.[6] In my previous book on sexual addiction, those who suffer from unwanted behaviours often seek comfort in the commonly quoted Serenity Prayer written by the American theologian Rein-

---

6. Ying Chen, Tyler J VanderWeele, Associations of Religious Upbringing With Subsequent Health and Well-Being From Adolescence to Young Adulthood: An Outcome-Wide Analysis, *American Journal of Epidemiology*, Volume 187, Issue 11, November 2018, Pages 2355–2364, https://doi.org/10.1093/aje/kwy142

hold Niebuhr and practised in recovery programs like AA.[7] The prayer asks God to help you change what you can, accept what you cannot, and have the wisdom to know the difference. St. Augustine famously declared, "Patience is the companion of wisdom."[8] Yet despite life's many challenges, we find courage, strength, and hope in facing them through waiting patiently on God. We see evidence of this throughout Psalms, particularly in verse 40:1-3 (NIV):

> *I waited patiently for the Lord;*
> *and he inclined to me, and heard my cry.*
> *He brought me up out of the pit of*
>   *destruction,*
> *out of the miry clay;*
> *And he set my feet upon a rock,*
> *making my footsteps firm.*
> *And he put a new song in my mouth,*
> *a song of praise to our God;*
> *Many will see and fear,*
> *And will trust in the Lord.*

Waiting is part and parcel of the Christian life. The heart of one who is patient with God is not listless. What rings true in the Psalms is that David carries a sense of

---

7. https://en.wikipedia.org/wiki/Reinhold_Niebuhr
8. The Theological Epistemology of Augustine's De trinitate (Oxford: Oxford University Press, 2008), PG

humility and hope throughout the act of waiting. He is calm in approach even though he's fervent in his plea. He's practising the act of patience through prayer without resorting to frustration. He doesn't know when God will answer, but he meets God diligently by showing up and finding courage and strength.

When genuine faith resides in an individual, it enables the believer to "rest in the Lord and wait patiently for Him" (v. 7; NASB; NKJV).[9]

Despite life's many difficulties, the believer finds courage and strength to meet them in waiting on the Lord, for "God is our strong refuge" (Psalm. 46:1).[10]

Of course, I'm not implying that one should pray and everything will be Jim-dandy. Faith enables trust and rest in the Lord so that you can wait patiently for Him. Only then can you have a realistic perspective on life's issues, knowing that God's plan will ultimately be done and faith in Him will be rewarded. However, prayer is also an act of humbly surrendering on a bended knee that weighs you down. Philip Yancey writes in his book on Prayer,

> "My Prayers are essentially selfish, an effort to employ God to help me accomplish my ends. I look on God as a problem-solver (a weed-puller) while overlooking the striking evidence of God's work all around me. And

---

9. Richard D. Patterson, "Rest in Troublesome Times," Biblical Studies Press (2014), 6.
10. "The Source of True Strength," Biblical Studies Press, 2013. https://bible.org/article/source-true-strength

when nothing much seems to happen, I grow impatient. There is a cure for impatience in prayer, I have found: Keep praying. You will likely grow so frustrated that you will either give up the practice or change your approach to prayer. Jean Nicolas Grou, a mystic from the eighteenth century, prescribed that healthy prayer should be humble, reverent, loving, confident and persevering — in other words, the exact opposite of impatient. I like to see the results of my labours. I work on an article and several months later it appears in print. I climb a mountain and reach the summit. Prayer operates by different rules, God's rules. We do it in secret, so that no one notices the effort, and the results — God's results, not ours — come in surprising ways, often long after we expected them. Prayer means opening myself to God and not limiting God through my own preconceptions. In sum, prayer means letting God be God."[11]

Whether we talk to God while walking, kneeling at the foot of our bed, or writing to Him in our journals, prayer has calming and positive attributes of well-being and a positive impact on mental health, as pointed out earlier. Prayer is a step to shutting out the world, patiently waiting and listening — it is impossible to arrive at a list of

---

11. Yancey, Philip. Prayer. United Kingdom: Hodder & Stoughton, 2011.

demands that require immediate responses. If anything teaches you the skill of patience, prayer does.

Wisdom in Waiting

No greater thing is created suddenly, any more than a bunch of grapes or a fig. If you tell me that you desire a fig, I answer you that there must be time. Let it first blossom, then bear fruit, then ripen.

— Epictetus

THE PEARL OF WISDOM, OFTEN CHALLENGING, HAS historically tested many great leaders, requiring them to exercise profound patience. Growing up in apartheid South Africa, I knew of a man who became emblematic of such wisdom and patience, though I knew him only from the annals of history. At the time, I didn't fully grasp the extent of his influence. His name carried significant weight across the colour lines in the nation of my birth and, eventually, worldwide. This man was Nelson Mandela, regarded as the father of modern-day South Africa. He dedicated his life to fighting for equal opportunities, embodying the struggle for freedom from the oppressive shackles of political tyranny—a cause he was willing to die for. This resolve is immortalised in his autobiography, Long Walk to Freedom, a copy of which remains a constant presence on my bookshelf. Mandela would spend the next twenty-seven years incarcerated — a large part of which involved the menial, backbreaking task of sitting in the prison yard smashing rocks into gravel with a hammer.

Mandela's biography is not just a tale of personal endurance; it reflects the broader narrative of a nation grappling with profound change. During the latter part of my high school years, I witnessed the beginning of this transformation. Having spent most of my educational years in an all-white institution, the gradual introduction of black students marked a significant turning point. These changes at a micro level mirrored the seismic shifts about to sweep across the nation. As Mandela's release loomed — a moment we all sensed was both inevitable and historic — my friends and I found ourselves on the cusp of witnessing the dawn of the 'rainbow nation.' However, this transition was not devoid of challenges. While many celebrated, a significant portion of the white community was consumed by fear and anxiety, troubled by the prospect of civil unrest. As South Africa teetered on the brink, I saw many families, including those of close friends, leave the country in anticipation of the changes to come. Internationally, there was a collective sense of anxious anticipation about how Mandela would navigate the nation through these turbulent times. Mandela's journey to becoming an iconic figure of global reverence was characterised by immense patience and resilience. Initially marked by a genuine desire for immediate change, his long imprisonment taught him the virtues of patience and contemplation. Reflecting on his incarceration, Mandela noted,

> "Prison itself is a tremendous education in the need for patience and perseverance. It is above all a test of one's commitment."[1]

He had a lot of time to think and learned composure through routine and mundanity. He never squandered or wallowed in self-pity and frustration in the moments he did have to himself. It was a period of intense learning and reflection. He became an avid reader, pursued studies in law, and, most notably, learned Afrikaans—the language of his oppressors. This strategic choice allowed him to better communicate with prison officials and later negotiate effectively with the architects of apartheid. His proficiency in Afrikaans was initially met with disdain by

---

1. Nelson Mandela (2012). "Notes to the Future: Words of Wisdom", p.37, Simon and Schuster Venter, Sahm., Hatang, S. K.., Abrams, Douglas B.., Mandela, Nelson. Notes to the Future: Words of Wisdom. United States: Atria Books, 2012.

younger activists, who remembered the forced imposition of the language during the 1976 uprising. But Mandela was clear on his position: to understand and win the enemy over, you must know their language, their passions, hopes and fears. In an interview with Oprah Winfrey, she asked him what lesson he had learned that carried through with him today when reflecting on his twenty-seven years in prison. His Xhosa accent is so distinct that I can almost imagine him answering it with soft, clipped pauses:

> "That principle influenced me throughout my life. I learned to have the patience to listen when people put forward their views, even if I think those views are wrong. You can't reach a just decision in a dispute unless you listen to both sides, ask questions, and view the evidence placed before you. If you don't allow people to contribute, to offer their point of view, or to criticise what has been put before them, then they can never like you. And you can never build that instrument of collective leadership."[2]

Mandela's embodiment of patience was pivotal when he was finally released. For twenty-seven years, he was denied gratification for experiencing true freedom. He tapped into the deep insights gained from years of reflec-

---

2. This interview appeared in the April 2001 issue of O, The Oprah Magazine. Read more: https://www.oprah.com/world/oprah-interviews-nelson-mandela/all#ixzz6mwwwH5jg

tion and dialogue to foster peace and reconciliation, steering South Africa from the brink of civil war and towards a democratic future. His wisdom, deeply rooted in his experiences and the philosophical teachings he encountered, did not arise spontaneously but was a testament to years of growth and understanding.

Mandela was akin to a modern-day Stoic. During his imprisonment, he was secretly handed a copy of Marcus Aurelius's *Meditations*—a seminal work containing the Roman emperor's personal reflections and Stoic philosophies. This book ignited Mandela's deeper appreciation for wisdom, drawing from the rich traditions of Hellenistic philosophy. The Hellenic era was prolific in producing sage thinkers, notably the Greek Stoic philosopher Epictetus, who profoundly articulated the virtues of patience and mental maturity. His words resonated deeply with him:

> "Nothing important comes into being overnight; even grapes or figs need time to ripen. If you say that you want a fig now, I will tell you to be patient. First, you must allow the tree to flower, then put forth fruit; then you have to wait until the fruit is ripe. So if the fruit of a fig tree is not brought to maturity instantly or in an hour, how do you expect the human mind to come to fruition, so quickly and easily?"[3]

---

3. Discourses I, 15.7–8 (Epictetus)

These ancient principles underscore the universal truth that meaningful change requires time and patience, applicable both to the natural world and human societies. This perspective resonates through the annals of history, influencing not just philosophers but kings, queens, soldiers, and scientists, and even the messianic teachings of Jesus Christ.

With its sweet, honeyed flavour, the fig has flavoured our cuisine and history, witnessing and shaping the human story. Native to the sunny and arid climates of the Mediterranean and the Middle East, the fig tree was one of the first fruit trees to be cultivated. Its fruit is notorious for its slow ripening process. Under stress, such as extreme weather or water scarcity, a fig tree might halt ripening altogether, entering a self-preservation mode to protect its seeds. The maturation of figs parallels a parable from Jesus, who used the budding of a fig tree to impart lessons of wisdom and patience (Matt 24:32–35; Mark 13:28–29; Luke 21:29–31). His simple yet profound parable would have been easily understood by his disciples, illustrating that just as the fig tree signals the approaching summer harvest, so too was the nearness of God's Kingdom and the second coming of Christ. Jesus employed this natural

---

Discourses and Selected Writings. United Kingdom: Penguin Books Limited, 2008

metaphor to emphasise that faith, like the fruit, requires time to develop fully—an exercise in patience and an emblem of faithful living. The fig tree, symbolic of Israel, became a metaphor for the faithful anticipation and patient cultivation of one's spirit, awaiting God's timing.

The Bible abounds with narratives where wisdom fosters patience in those willing to embrace it, contrasting sharply with tales where impatience breeds folly. Notable biblical figures were endowed with exceptional wisdom, which guided nations and shaped histories. Joseph received divine wisdom that impressed Pharaoh, leading to his appointment as governor over Egypt (Acts 7:10). Moses, educated in all the wisdom of the Egyptians, was influential in speech and action (Acts 7:20-22). Joshua was imbued with wisdom when Moses laid hands on him, earning him the trust and obedience of the Israelites (Deut 34:9). During Nebuchadnezzar's reign, Daniel was recognised for his extraordinary insight and god-like wisdom (Daniel 5:11-12).

Solomon, perhaps the epitome of wisdom, was granted a profound understanding that it surpassed all the sages of the East and Egypt (1 Kings 4:29). His wisdom, celebrated through three thousand proverbs and one thousand and five songs, drew kings from distant lands to hear his insights. Yet, despite the breadth of his wisdom, Solomon's later years were marred by decisions that led to his spiritual downfall, illustrating that wisdom can be fleeting and must be continually cultivated (1 Kings 11:1-8).

These stories underscore a crucial distinction: knowing is not synonymous with possessing wisdom. Knowledge without application is inert, whereas wisdom activates knowledge through discernment and action. Adam's story in the Garden of Eden is a testament to this principle; despite his perfect knowledge, his failure to apply it wisely led to consequences humanity still endure.

Our lives are replete with moments where we must choose between wisdom and folly. When faced with parental advice or societal rules, do we listen or rebel based on our limited understanding? Wisdom is not merely about accumulating knowledge but applying it judiciously and patiently in our decisions.

The Oxford Dictionary defines wisdom as "the ability to make sensible decisions and give good advice because of the experience and knowledge that you have." True wisdom combines knowledge with the patience to see things through, to wait for the right moment, and to act with consideration. It is the person who holds their tongue, the leader who listens, the entrepreneur who seeks counsel—a testament to the proverb, "He who knowledge spares his words, and a man of understanding is of calm spirit. Even a fool is counted wise when he holds his peace; when he shuts his lips, he is considered perceptive" (Proverbs 17:27-28 NKJV).

As we navigate the complexities of life, wisdom calls us to discern, pause, and consider deeply. It invites us to cultivate a calm spirit, delay gratification, and deliberate thoughtfully before acting. This journey of wisdom enriches our lives and moulds our character, shaping us into individuals who can genuinely make a difference in the world.

The Formation of Character

Two things define you: Your patience when you have nothing and your attitude when you have everything.

— George Bernard Shaw

WHEN I WAS A CHILD, I HAD A SATURDAY MORNING ritual. Rain or shine, I'd sprint to the end of the driveway to retrieve the weekend newspaper, always encased in a plastic bag, knotted tightly at the end. On my way back to the house, I'd quickly wipe off any grit, tear open the plastic, and excitedly announce to my dad, "The paper's here!" I was always the first to grab the entertainment section named Tonight. I'd find a cozy spot on the carpet where sunlight formed a warm patch, lie down with my head cradled in my hands and my skinny legs waving, and dive into the cartoon strips. World events like the fall of the Berlin Wall, the invasion of Kuwait, or Nelson Mandela's release — though monumental — were just background noise to me. Instead, the antics of Calvin & Hobbes filled my world, a comic strip I adored. Despite being six years older than Calvin, I found a kindred spirit in his youthful escapades. I had imaginary friends, too, though none as vivid as an anthropomorphic tiger named after the philosopher Thomas Hobbes.

I noticed a recurring theme in the comic strip as I read more. Calvin's habitual resistance, his frequent misunderstandings, and his failed attempts to grasp adult concepts always elicited the same response from his father: "It builds character." There's one strip where Calvin furiously shovels snow, getting increasingly frustrated at the slow progress. He shouts back at his house, questioning why they couldn't buy a snowblower like everyone else. His dad's voice counters from the open back door, "It builds character. Keep at it".[1]

Calvin always needed clarification on what building character meant. For him, the lure of immediate gratification and ease was far more appealing than the arduous path of character development. This mirrors a larger truth about patience: it involves enduring suffering. Patience means accepting or tolerating delays, problems, or suffering without annoyance or anxiety. It's fundamentally about endurance, which often consists of experiencing

---

1. Calvin and Hobbes by Bill Watterson for January 02, 1989

discomfort or pain—something we naturally try to avoid at all costs. Yet, enduring these trials is critical to developing maturity and character. In his perpetual state of childhood, Calvin never aged or evolved past these lessons but instead reflected a common desire to remain in a state of childlike bliss rather than face the challenges required to build character.

In a broader Christian context, patience is vital to spiritual and personal growth. The Apostle Paul, in his epistles, frequently encouraged Christians to practice patience, highlighting it as a fundamental aspect of living a life of faith. He explained that patience was a virtue and a necessary part of the Christian journey, particularly in dealing with others. "God will repay each person according to what they have done: to those who by patience in well-doing seek for glory and honour and immortality, he will give eternal life; but for those who are self-seeking and do not obey the truth, but obey unrighteousness, there will be wrath and fury" (Romans 2:6-8 NIV).[2] The word patience or endurance in some texts in Greek refers to hupomoné — the act of holding out. Paul knows it won't be easy for them, but he encourages the church in Rome to wait and practice this skill.[3] If they choose to abandon seeking

---

2. Psalm 62:12; Prov. 24:12
3. Strong, James. "G5281 - hupomoné - Strong's Greek Lexicon (KJV)

immediate self-gratification, rewards will come. I mention this because there's an exciting correlation throughout the New Testament. Hupomoné embodies many translated meanings — perseverance to endurance — all attributes of the act of patience.

This notion of patience interweaves with several other vital biblical concepts, such as tribulation, faith, hope, and joy. Tribulation fosters perseverance through rejoicing in it (Romans 5:3; 2 Corinthians 6:4). The Thessalonians were commendable for "holding out" during times of affliction (2 Thessalonians 1:4). In addressing the twelve dispersed tribes of the church, James refers to the patience of Job, a story all too familiar with enduring pain and suffering, sharing in his anguish and wonderment (James 5:11). Faith is another related word. James outlines this in the familiar verse where faith produces patience in times of testing (James 1:3). Hope is often referred to in verses like Romans 8:25. Despite not immediately seeing things play out, we can rest in hope. Patience and perseverance give us the tools to do that. Paul stresses that the promise leads to hope, which does not disappoint "because the love of God has been poured out in our hearts by the Holy Spirit who was given to us" (Romans 5:3-5 NKJV). Finding hope and comfort in the scriptures eases patience and endurance (Romans 15:4). Lastly, joy. The Christian walk compels us to be forever thankful and to revel in joy amid many life difficulties, hardships, and trials (James 1:3; Colossians 1:11-12). Our path will narrow as we continue to turn towards the cross and follow Christ. As such, trials and tribulations are inevitable. Patience is essential if we are to experience any triumph. Through these trials, our faith will get fitter. The more 'faith-fit' we become, the more hope and joy will abound. Our eyes remain fixed on Him, and we look forward to the glory of being together.

In the biblical narrative, patience intricately weaves into the fabric of God's sovereignty. Although His grace abounds, complete sanctification in this life isn't guaranteed. Patience, therefore, is not just a virtue to be willed into existence but a divine gift we are called to cultivate, enabled by the Holy Spirit working within us to make us more Christ-like.

The Bible is replete with accounts of men and women whose faith and character were profoundly tested through patience. Noah dedicated his entire life to building an ark, dwelling aboard it for three hundred and seventy-eight days, steadfast in his patience for God's promise of a new land (Genesis 7-8). Abraham, called to be the father of many nations, waited until he was a hundred years old before the promise of a son with Sarah was fulfilled (Genesis 21:5). In similar trials of patience, Rebekah, after marrying Isaac, found herself barren and waited twenty years before giving birth to twins, enduring in faith (Genesis 25:21).

Joseph's journey is another testament to patience; from dreaming of leadership to being sold into slavery and unjustly imprisoned, he held fast to God's timing, rising to become the governor of Egypt (Genesis 37-41). Jacob also demonstrated patience, labouring for fourteen years to marry Rachel, the woman he loved (Genesis 29:18-30). Job's endurance is legendary, as he maintains faith in God's goodness despite severe trials and losses (Job 1-42).

Other biblical figures illustrate the virtue of patience in their walks with God. Daniel remained steadfast and patient even when faced with the lion's den, trusting in God's deliverance (Daniel 6). Hosea's patience was shown in his love for his unfaithful wife, reflecting God's patience with Israel (Hosea 1-3). Esther's fast for three days before approaching the king demonstrated her patience and strategic timing in saving her people (Esther 4-5). Moses led the Israelites through the desert for forty years, constantly facing their complaints and disbelief, yet he patiently guided them to the Promised Land (Exodus and Numbers). Similarly, Caleb waited patiently until he was eighty-five to receive his portion of the land he had scouted as a young man (Joshua 14:10). In her deep yearning for a child, Hannah exemplified patience through fervent prayer and faith, eventually dedicating her son Samuel to God's service (1 Samuel 1). The Apostle Paul, who endured hardships like beatings and shipwrecks during his missionary journeys, frequently encouraged the early Church to embrace patience as a reflection of their faith and love (2 Corinthians 6:4, Romans 5:3-5). Jesus Himself, the cornerstone of the Christian faith, embodied patience in His ministry and passion, culminating in His crucifixion and resurrection. His life and teachings underscore the necessity of patience in the face of trials and tribulations (Matthew, Mark, Luke, and John).

The Biblical narrative champions patience as a divine command and showcases it as integral to the Christian character, essential for spiritual growth and maturity. This narrative arc from Genesis to Revelation underscores that patience is intertwined with trust in God's timing and plan, reflecting the profound transformation within us, akin to the metamorphosis of a butterfly. Patience allows for a transformation that can be challenging. To forgive, hope, trust, love, lead, encourage and endure. To do this, we need to allow God to work through us in His timing (Isaiah 64:8 NKJV):

> *But now, O Lord,*
> *You are our Father;*
> *We are the clay, and You our potter;*
> *And all we are the work of Your hand.*

Such patience is not passive waiting but an active, disciplined participation in faith, leading to a more prosperous, spiritually aligned existence.

Patience is not optional within the Christian walk. The two go hand in hand. The apostle Paul reiterates for Christians to practice patience time and time again (1 Corinthians 13:4, 1 Thessalonians 5:14, Galatians 6:9, Romans 12:12, Ephesians 4:2, Romans 15:5). It is also the first thing he attributes to love. Showing patience is a fundamental litmus test of Christian authenticity. Christian character, evidence of a new creation, manifests in authentic patience.

Similarly, the life cycle of a butterfly provides a profound metaphor for understanding patience and transformation. Just as a caterpillar undergoes metamorphosis within the chrysalis, emerging as a butterfly, so does the Christian life require seasons of waiting and transformation. These waiting periods are not passive but active times of growth and change, preparing us for the roles God has in store for us. Without patience, we cannot fully develop the qualities necessary to fulfil God's purpose. Patience allows us to navigate through difficulties and challenges, moulding us into vessels that reflect God's love and grace to others.

Furthermore, patience reflects our trust in God's sovereignty and perfect timing. It acknowledges that we are not in control, but rather, we are part of a divine plan that unfolds according to God's will. This trust in God's timing can be challenging, especially when we face trials and tribulations. However, through these experiences, our faith is strengthened, and our character is refined. Just as gold is purified in the fire, so too are we purified through the trials that test our patience and endurance.

The practice of patience also extends to our interactions with others. Patience can seem countercultural in a world that often values instant gratification and quick results.

However, as Christians, we are called to embody patience in our relationships, showing grace and understanding to those around us. This patience is not passive but active, seeking to understand and support others even when difficult. Through patience, we can build strong, lasting relationships that reflect the love of Christ.

The story of Job is a powerful example of patience in the face of suffering. Despite losing everything—his wealth, health, and family—he remained steadfast in his faith. He did not understand why he was suffering but trusted God's sovereignty and remained patient. Ultimately, God restored Job's fortunes, blessing him even more than he had before. Job's story teaches us that patience in the face of suffering is a testament to our faith and trust in God. Through patience, we can endure the trials of life and emerge stronger in our faith.

Patience is also essential in our spiritual growth and development. It allows us to wait on God's timing, trusting He knows what is best for us. This waiting is not passive but active, involving prayer, study of the Scriptures, and seeking God's will in our lives. We can develop a deeper relationship with God through patience and understanding His character and plans. As we grow in patience, we become more attuned to the leading of the Holy Spirit, allowing us to walk in step with God's will. Patience is a vital virtue in the Christian life. We can endure trials, develop our character, and grow our faith through patience. Patience allows us to trust God's timing and plans for our lives, even when we do not understand them. We can reflect Christ's love and grace to those around us through patience and building strong, lasting relationships. As we cultivate patience, we become more Christ-like, embodying the virtues essential to our spiritual growth and maturity. Let us strive to develop patience, trusting in God's timing and His perfect plan for our lives, knowing that it is through patience that we can truly reflect the love and grace of Christ.

Waiting for God

> I am sure that God keeps no one waiting unless He sees that it is good for him to wait.
>
> — C.S Lewis

As Christians, "Waiting on the Lord" is commonly bandied about as a catch-all remedy for life's decisions and desires, from choosing a spouse to acquiring a Mustang. In my household, it's humorously applied to hopes of our national rugby team winning a trophy. However, this saying should be used more often.

Waiting earnestly involves repeatedly bringing our prayers and supplications to God, especially when they seem unanswered or lost in a void. This practice becomes more challenging when outcomes are beyond our control and we are uncertain of God's involvement. Oswald Chambers insightfully remarked, "One of the greatest strains in life is the strain of waiting for God," highlighting the spiritual and emotional challenge it entails. Henri Nouwen expands this concept:

> "... in which we live the present moment to the full in order to find there the signs of the One we are waiting for. Waiting patiently always means paying attention to what is happening right before our eyes and seeing there the first rays of God's glorious coming."[1]

Waiting on the Lord itself sounds heavy with gravitas, as if we're waiting for a divine message hand-delivered by cherubim, written on a papyrus scroll in the finest calligraphy, sealed with a wax emblem by God Himself. Over the years, I've realised that waiting on Him isn't just a model or a stance to adopt; it's gaining an intimate knowledge of His patience. How is God patient with us? How does He show His patience? Indeed, the message of God's promises fulfilled and His Kingdom restored is a story of patience. We see this theme of endurance throughout the Old Testament. From the dawn of time, God was slow to anger. He demonstrated patience when Adam and Eve sinned, marked by their long road from the Garden of Eden. He covered their naked bodies and shame and

---

1. Nouwen, Henri J. M.. Here and Now: Living in the Spirit. United Kingdom: Crossroad Publishing Company, 2001, pg 31

promised redemption through a saviour (Genesis 3:15). God also "... patiently waited in the days of Noah while the ark was being built" (1 Peter 3:20 NET). Noah warned of a flood despite people having never seen rain. Millions perished in the flood for refusing Noah's counsel and ignoring God's command. Only eight people survived: Noah, his three sons, and their wives. According to Genesis 6:3, God gave them one hundred and twenty years. His warning to generations could not have been more apparent or more generous. Yet, despite God's patience, only eight willingly responded. Millions rejected God and perished in that first civilisation. Again, God showed His patience toward Abraham, through whom all the world's Gentiles are blessed, becoming like the "sand of the seashore, which cannot be counted" (Genesis 22:17). God even introduced His attribute of patience to Moses through His name. "And he passed in front of Moses, proclaiming, 'The Lord, the Lord, the compassionate and gracious God, slow to anger, abounding in love and faithfulness, maintaining love to thousands, and forgiving wickedness, rebellion, and sin'" (Exodus 34:6-7 NIV). Moses needed to hear this. Although he was the meekest man on earth (Numbers 12:3), he was clearly at his wit's end. Imagine being a leader, and no one listens to you. After everything he did for his people, they made a golden calf and worshipped it, believing it had brought them out of Egypt. Imagine witnessing some of the daft things they did.

In his impatience, Moses smashed the tablets bearing

the Ten Commandments that God had given him. But God showed immense patience despite Israel's impatience. He sees all we do and restrains Himself to allow time for repentance, even when we deserve death. God could have quickly asserted His superiority and told the Israelites to return to Egypt if they wanted. He could have justly done anything, but the scripture tells us He is slow to anger. We see God's patience stretched time and again. In Nehemiah's time, Moses appeals to God similarly after the Babylonian captivity. He urges God to do what He has done before. "But You are God, ready to pardon, gracious and merciful, slow to anger, abundant in kindness, and did not forsake them" (Nehemiah 9:17 NKJV). David, a man after God's heart, also had continuous shortcomings. Yet again, God proved He was in it for the long haul and showed patience with David and Israel. God demonstrated His patience through the words of His prophets (James 5:10). Throughout the Old Testament, God kept His promises and covenant with Israel. For a nation deserving of His wrath, God exercised long-suffering, patience, and forbearance (Romans 9:22-23). In the New Testament, Jesus Christ often showed God's patient character toward sinners and in His work of salvation. We see this displayed in His interactions with people, His disciples' teachings, and the long-suffering journey to the cross. Paul emphasises this in Timothy, "But here is why I was treated with mercy: so that in me, as the worst, Christ Jesus could demonstrate his utmost patience, as an example for those who are going to believe in him for eternal life" (1 Timothy 1:16). In James 5:7-11, he calls for patience amidst suffering, to hold out for the second coming of Christ and how we ought to respond. He references Job as a perfect example of steadfastness.

All in God's perfect timing. The day and the hour are known only to the Lord, even though we do not know. We cannot set the date, but we can persevere. It still rings true today as it did then. More time has passed, but a day unto God is a thousand years, and a thousand years is a day. He is long-suffering toward people who want to come to Him from every nation, tribe, tongue, and people. As a Christian, it is abundantly clear how much we owe everything to His patience and mercy. Despite our tendency to repeat historical mistakes rather than learn from them, Albert Barnes affirms this beautifully in his commentary:

> "God bears with people from childhood to youth; from youth to manhood; from manhood to old age; often while they violate every law, contemn his mercy, profane his name, and disgrace their species; and still, notwithstanding all this, his anger is turned away, and the sinner lives, and "riots in the beneficence of God." If there is anything that can affect the heart of man, it is this; and when he is brought to see it, and contemplate it, it rushes over the soul and overwhelms it with bitter sorrow."

> "The mercy and forbearance of God are constant. The manifestations of his goodness come in every form; in the

sun, and light, and air; in the rain, the stream, the dew-drop; in food, and raiment, and home; in friends, and liberty, and protection; in health, and peace; and in the gospel of Christ, and the offers of life; and in all these ways God is appealing to his creatures each moment. and setting before them the evils of ingratitude, and beseeching them to turn and live.[2]

God's promises are always consistent, even when His timing is far from rushed. The biblical timeline suggests hundreds of years between epochs, displaying God's enduring patience. How often did Abraham and Moses pray to God, asking Him to spare His anger towards Israel? God never wavered; man did. Most of us see patience or lack thereof from the Israelites' perspective. If we see it from God's point of view, He is not slow in keeping His promises, as we might understand slowness to mean. As the apostle Peter tells us, "The Lord is not slow concerning his promise, as some regard slowness, but is being patient toward you, because he does not wish for any to perish but for all to come to repentance" (2 Peter 3:9 NET). That is the whole point of the gospel: God's kingdom is fulfilled in Christ so that we are ALL saved. I have yet to find a more significant example of a book other than the Bible as the ultimate test of man's patience and

---

2. Notes on the Bible, by Albert Barnes, [1834], at sacred-texts.com 3 and 4
   https://www.sacred-texts.com/bib/cmt/barnes/rom002.htm

trust in God's timing. I'm still determining what will happen if that doesn't illustrate it enough and provide hope. It's evident His timing, more often than not, is different from ours. Our lives exist within time; some of us are conscious of our mortality, so we approach life in a hurry. God doesn't exist in time and space as we perceive. His celestial clock is set to a much bigger timeline and picture. Rushing is not in God's vocabulary or character. "Only I can tell you the future before it even happens. Everything I plan will come to pass, for I do whatever I wish" (Isaiah 46:10 NLT). God already knows what tomorrow brings. Reading the Bible is an act of discipline and patience in itself. Understanding God's view on patience, one realises is a greater priority for God than for us.

Patience is a part of God's character; it's who He is connecting with us. Conversely, it's also a learned grace part of Christian character development. When the Bible speaks of God's patience, it does so as forbearance or long-suffering. It's essential to understand and examine these two distinctions:

Forbearance

Forbearance is not a commonplace word in today's vocabulary. It is a basic form of patience. We associate it with self-control, restraint, and tolerance in today's language. It is a relatively short-term action of tolerance aimed at a person or group because of some wrongdoing, perceived or otherwise, against us. In a biblical context, it has quite the opposite meaning. Reading the Scriptures comes from a place of love or motivation by indignation. Turning to the Greek Lexicon, we start to see broader strokes. Forbearance sits comfortably alongside the synonyms: 'self-restraint,' 'to tolerate,' or 'to put up with.' When zooming in on the Greek word in context to particular verses, a clearer picture of God's intent forms. Forbearance — ἀνοχῆς (anochēs); reveals His 'holding-in' or 'restraining His indignation'; or 'forbearing to manifest His displeasure against sin. Understanding God's 'forbearance' reveals His intention in exercising patience, allowing humanity to grasp both the penalty for sin and the contrasting hope found in His plan to redeem us by paying the price for our sins. The dichotomy between displeasure and mercy is the high standard of God. It goes far beyond a surface-level practice of patience. Although forbearance lives more in the dictionary than on our lips, it's practicable. Like God, we too can show forbearance when sinned against — slander, wrongdoings, hate, gossip towards others, to name a few. Forbearance is part of the Christian walk but doesn't presuppose ease. As Paul famously said, "We are fools for Christ's sake, but you are wise in Christ! We are weak, but you are strong! You are distinguished, but we are dishonoured! To the present hour, we both hunger and thirst, and we are poorly clothed and beaten and homeless. And we labour, working with our own hands. Being reviled, we bless; being persecuted, we endure; being defamed, we entreat" (1 Corinthians 4:10-13 NIV). In verse 12 *endure* in Greek is *anechó*, meaning 'still bearing: up, to persist, to forbear'. In this sense, Paul is making it clear that when persecuted, we hold ourselves from reacting, and we 'put up' with it. We restrain ourselves.[3]

How many of us hold back when someone says something hurtful about us? How many of us immediately lash out and argue? Paul wasn't superhuman. He was like you and I. I doubt he would've bitten his top lip at times, but he could "forbear." He understood the cost of what it meant to be Christ-like (steward in). All of these are necessary experiences that shape the Christian character. Paul starts the chapter by saying that "as stewards of Christ," it is required that we "...be found faithful". "Having forbearance" towards others is part of being "stewards" in Christ. We have a responsibility as Christians to express the attribute as God did with us. Moses is a good example. Considered faithful, he often needed the 'knack' for the patience Paul talks about. Here's a man who has been put through the wringer with the Israelites repeatedly. He 'put up' with their complaining and grumbling for forty years when they lacked faith in the promise. Forty years is enough to break anyone. Think about it the next time your

---

3. Hocking, D. "The Patience of God by David Hocking." Blue Letter Bible. Last Modified 11 Aug, 2010. https://www.blueletterbible.org/Comm/hocking_david/attributes/attributes14.cfm

WiFi goes down. He's forgiven for his outbursts and the consequences of his flesh getting the better of him. Yet despite the low and regrettable moments, he's remembered as a steward for God's people. God saw him as a faithful servant (Hebrews 11:23-29), and the price he paid is a lesson from God on forbearance. It's easy to react when you're feeling weary and beaten down — God understands this. He also wants us to read Moses' life as a lesson. To heed his word, to keep pressing on. The Christian walk is an exercise of grace through faith and perseverance. The more we practice patience, the more 'forbearance' will direct us — the journey leading us to a place of long-suffering.

Long-Suffering

Similar in meaning and function to forbearance, long-suffering is more interchangeable than supposed. Although there's delineation, it's less about application in the immediate moment or circumstance. It is a character quality developed over time through many similar experiences. Time is the critical differentiator.

The Greek transliteration makrothumía suggests longanimity, long-tempered, slow to anger, divinely-regulated patience, and slow to wrath. As a compound word, it's worth looking at the individual sums. 'Macro' means distant, far, long duration, rooted in time. Thymós'/'thumós' means an outburst of passion, anger, wrath—rooted in behaviour. It can refer to one's essence with one's soul or spirit. Often, an emotional response and why 'thumós' can mean heart. In other words, to go long before exercising a personal reaction or behaviour. It's less about being patient for good things to come. Instead, patient application and endurance of wrongdoings strengthen through his glorious power. Upon closer observation, I discovered that *makrothumia* is a feminine noun. It is perhaps fitting to why women are less likely to be physically aggressive. They have higher pain thresholds and seemingly endure things longer. From childbearing to childbirth, I can testify to my wife exercising long-suffering.

In Romans 2:4 (NKJV), Paul paints a surprising connection between forbearance and long-suffering when speaking of God, "Or do you despise the riches of His goodness, forbearance, and long-suffering, not knowing that the goodness of God leads you to repentance?" Both words are a product of "His goodness"— mutually exclusive yet exercised in harmony. The apostle addresses the judgmental attitude in Romans 1 and implies that they can't have their cake and eat it. He's somewhat dumbfounded by their presumptuous attitude. They acknowledge God's goodness yet think they are exempt from His merciful warnings and punishment of sin. This miscalculation is true for those who often mistake kindness for weakness. God's displeasure against and slowness to react doesn't absolve punishment of sin. Instead, He offers time and opportunity to turn away from it. Indeed, God has the qualities of exercising forbearance (in instances of disobedience) and long-suffering (holding back his wrath and displeasure). In essence, this is "the riches of his goodness." Paul recognises these two qualities of God intend to bring all sinners, you and I, to repentance.

I use the above example because it is comparable to Exodus 34:6-7. God proclaims His qualities as "merciful and gracious, long-suffering, and abundant in goodness and truth." No other nation experienced and received patience in such biblical proportions. God's long-suffering with Israel through the promise of His kingdom outlined in the Old and New is a testament to his enduring patience. Some Jews who repented and welcomed the fulfilled promise of the Kingdom through Christ saw the benefit of the long-suffering of God. Those who rejected the Messiah saw the destruction of the temple, followed by years under Roman rule. The bigger story, though, is not about one nation's demise—instead, the promise of the New Covenant and the lessons learned. The recovery of Israel's triumph was God's long-suffering.

As Christians, we are to emulate the very patience of God, "...who will render to each one according to his deeds: eternal life to those who by patient continuance in doing good seek for glory, honour, and immortality..."(Romans 2:6-7 NKJV). If history has taught us anything, God's patience is never impulsive. It is a display of self-possessed capacity for calm over a long period (Romans 9:22). It is an attribute that never overlooks justice and punishment but is imminent and fair. Despite our sinful nature, He gives us countless opportunities and encouragement to repent. He is incredibly patient with us, not wanting anyone to perish (Ezekiel 18:23, 32; 33:11; 1 Timothy 2:3; 2 Peter 3:9). The great irony is we often plead to God for more time 'to come right'. "If you give me one more chance, I will...", "Just let me see this through to the end, and I will...". Yet, how much more do we restrain our anger before we crack? A father who is abusive, a wayward son, a hurtful friend — how long are we prepared to wait patiently? The pain of waiting can point our hearts to the life-saving patience of God. We owe our everything to His kindness and patience with us.

Part Three
Acts Of Patience

Harvesting the Fourth Fruit

Patience is bitter, but it's fruit is sweet.

— Jean Jaques Roussouw

One guilty pleasure of mine, which my wife considers more of a punishment, is my love for spicy food. I seize every opportunity to add some heat to my meals. Finding a bottle of hot sauce next to my dinner plate each evening is commonplace. Most Saturday evenings, you can find me preparing an Indian curry for myself while the rest of my family opts for pizza. I even go as far as adding chilli honey to my Rooibos tea. Perched on the windowsill next to me is a Habanero plant I recently acquired from a garden centre. I hope it will yield enough peppers to make some great hot sauce—spicy yet flavorful without causing any alarm on the Scoville scale. It's positioned to catch the morning sun and serves as a reminder to water it every third day.

As I carefully tend to this plant, waiting for its fruits to mature, I am often reminded of a deeper metaphorical connection to patience. Much like the long wait for Habanero peppers to ripen, spiritual growth — specifically the "fruit of the spirit" described in Galatians 5:22-23 — requires time, care, and patience. Patience is listed as one of the spiritual fruits Paul describes. By definition, fruit results from two life-streams: the Lord living His life through ours and to yield what is eternal (1 John 4:17).[1] Just as tending a pepper plant demands precision and perseverance, developing spiritual fruit involves a similar process of cultivating inner qualities over time. In the same way that I must resist the urge to rush the growth of my Habanero plant, spiritual growth is not instant, and the results, much like the harvest, are worth waiting for.

When Paul uses the word "fruit" (Greek: karpós), he's not just referring to literal fruit but to outcomes of our actions — whether in character or crops. He likens personal development and spiritual virtues to slow, intentional cultivation. Just as harvesting peppers demands patience and precise timing, nurturing the fruits of the Spirit, such as patience, within ourselves takes time and

---

1. https://biblehub.com/greek/2590.htm. 2022 H.E.L.P.S. Ministries, Inc. a 501(c)3 non-profit and creators of The Discovery Bible. All Rights Reserved.

trust. Overwatering my plant risks its demise, as rushing character development can hinder spiritual growth. But when we abide, both in tending to our plants and in our relationship with Christ, the harvest, whether of peppers or patience, eventually comes.

The Theology of John Edwards notes that Paul viewed Christian virtues collectively as having beauty and symmetry: "There is a concatenation of the graces of Christianity. All the graces or virtues link together or unite one to another and within one another, as the links of a chain. One aspect of love is contained. In another it leads to a third, and so on".[2] Paul is not merely describing these virtues; he emphasises their interconnectedness. They are not isolated, each bound to its season and growth conditions; they all share the same essence from the same spiritual source. We can't simply choose to develop patience without expecting it to affect other virtues like kindness, gentleness, love, and self-control.

It's feasible to naturally possess a temperament inclined towards kindness or patience, perhaps more quickly than someone else, like a colleague or friend. However, embodying all these virtues through mere human effort is unattainable. One may cultivate particular virtues out of self-interest, as mentioned in previous chapters, or these traits start to form from a young age. Still, an

---

2. McClymond, Michael James., McClymond, Michael J.., McDermott, Gerald R.. The Theology of Jonathan Edwards. United Kingdom: Oxford University Press, USA, 2012.

utterly virtuous character can only form through the Spirit. As Timothy Keller says, "If one is missing the others can't be produced".[3] Consider kindness: how can one respond kindly to a belittling boss without a foundation of love? Kindness appears temporarily, but genuine, sustained kindness is impossible without love. Similarly, if everything seems peaceful at work, it isn't true peace if humility is absent. As Keller reminds us, true peace depends on humility: "Worry is basically arrogance, assuming you know best how life ought to proceed, but humility brings peace as it submits to the wisdom of God. So, real peace depends on humility. Any fruit that appears to exist independently of the others is deceptive, as they inherently rely on one another."[4]

The fruit of the Spirit are not mere human traits; they stem from a life rooted in faith and salvation, as Paul outlines in Galatians 5:16. He contrasts this with the desires of the flesh, shedding light on the difference between human nature and godly character. This transformation is not about adhering to the impulses of the flesh and law but about freedom in the Holy Spirit. Walking in the Spirit signifies that the Spirit resides within you, guiding your actions and decisions in a cohesive dance with your own spirit, moving in harmony.

Patience stems from deep spiritual roots in Christ. If a

---

3. Keller, Timothy. Galatians for You. United Kingdom: Good Book Company, 2013.
4. Keller, Timothy. *The Freedom of Self-Forgetfulness.* 10Publishing, 2012, 35.

branch is barren or attempts are made to attach fruit to a withered branch, the result is inevitable decay. This illustrates the health of the tree itself; signs of lifelessness indicate a deeper issue. Patience emerges from a mature relationship with Christ. Often, those new to faith try to produce abundant fruit quickly, reflecting a form of impatience that can lead to disillusionment and wandering from the path. Christ, understanding His followers well, uses agricultural parables to explain these spiritual truths, such as the parable of the sower:

> "Now the parable is this: The seed is the word of God. Those by the wayside are the ones who hear; then the devil comes and takes away the word out of their hearts, lest they should believe and be saved. But the ones on the rock are those who, when they hear, receive the word with joy; and these have no root, who believe for a while and in time of temptation fall away. Now the ones that fell among thorns are those who, when they have heard, go out and are choked with cares, riches, and pleasures of life, and bring no fruit to maturity. But the ones that fell on the good ground are those who, having heard the word with a noble and good heart, keep it and bear fruit with patience (Luke 8:11-15 NKJV)."

Patience is essential for spiritual growth, as indicated in this verse. It requires a softened, fertile heart ready for the word of God to take root and flourish over time. The scripture clearly states that patience is crucial for bearing all the fruit associated with the Gospel, also warning against the impatient heart. In verse 5, Jesus describes the seed falling by the wayside as "trampled or trodden down," focusing on those who hear the word often yet fail to understand. Their hearts, like a well-worn path, become compacted, making it difficult for anything to grow. Isaiah uses a similar metaphor, warning Israel of becoming a desolate vineyard:

"And now, please let me tell you what I will do to My vineyard: I will take away its hedge, and it shall be burned; and break down its wall, and it shall be trampled down. I will lay it waste; It shall not be pruned or dug, But there shall come up briers and thorns. I will also command the clouds That they rain no rain on it"(Isaiah 5:5-6).

The prophet's warning is clear: Israel is at risk of becoming a trampled vineyard, repeatedly hearing God's warnings yet failing to heed them. Jesus draws a parallel here with "wayside hearers," who reject the word of God instead of embracing and understanding it to produce fruitful outcomes. According to Strong's Exhaustive Concordance, the Greek word for trampled or trodden down, katapateó, translates to 'reject with disdain.' This reflects an attitude of superiority and pride, common among the impatient. These "wayside hearers" epitomize impatience, grabbing at life with a focus on immediate gratification, dismissing anything that requires deeper comprehension and reflection. This is precisely why Paul prefaces his discussion on the fruits of the Spirit with a warning in Galatians 5:16: "So I say, walk by the Spirit, and you will not gratify the desires of the flesh." This highlights the importance of spiritual patience when faced with trials and temptations.

In our daily lives, resistance to patience when tested reveals much about our spiritual state. Paul calls for a deep-rooted understanding of the word, which does not allow for whims and desires to sway us. Without taking the time to listen to God's word with a 'good and noble heart' and allowing it to bear fruit with patience, we seek the benefits without the commitment.

The fruit of the Spirit, encompassing long-suffering and forbearance, fundamentally reflects God's character. Patience is not an innate human trait; one cultivates it through walking in the Spirit, which empowers us to endure challenges such as slander, grievance, and malice. It fosters a temperament that avoids explosive outbursts and judgmental reactions. James encourages the early church to "count it all joy when you fall into various trials, knowing that the testing of your faith produces patience" (James 1:2-3 NKJV). Here, patience (hypomonēn) involves waiting for things to happen and stepping back during challenging times. Consider situations like workplace challenges, buying a house, or competing in a race—each tests our patience and is poorly served by impulsive reactions. Yet, when we walk in the Spirit, this very action cultivates patience (*makrothymia*) that enables us to 'forbear' one another in a manner free from judgment, gossip, retaliation, and intolerance.

Understanding this deep-rooted patience is to recognise the full spectrum of love manifesting through our lives, sprouting anew. Only a life transformed by the Spirit can genuinely produce such fruit. As Christians, we are to run the long race, avoiding quick fixes and focusing on eternal truths set before us. We aim our hearts not on earthly things but on the heavenly, willing to wait for the Lord's timing without knowing the exact moment.

Enduring Grace: The Interplay of Tolerance and Patience

> The only thing that isn't worthless: to live this life out truthfully and rightly. And be patient with those who don't.
>
> — Marcus Aurelius

My wife and I decided on a wooden kitchen play set for my daughter's second birthday. It had all the trimmings for her to play 'chef'—complete with kitchenware and appliances. She especially took to the microwave, disturbingly stuffing her toy dog inside. Even so, this wooden marvel promised hours of pretend cooking. Of course, being from Ikea also meant hours of DIY dad time. Painstakingly figuring out if (2b) fits into bracket (M), or is it a (W)? After all the effort, I managed to finish by 3 a.m.

Exhausted but elated, I flopped onto the bed with her gift nestled against the Christmas tree. On Christmas Day, she embraced her kitchen like a mini Jamie Oliver, tucking in straight from the pan. Watching my daughter potter about her kitchen most mornings was a joy. I would oblige her request to squat down and remain precariously seated on tiny chairs, usually reserved for her fluffy dog GiGi and friends. Still, I watched as she prepared breakfast, politely serving me a saucer of wooden sushi and a cup of wooden broccoli to wash it down. Who was I to refuse?

One afternoon, I surprised her by picking her up from daycare early, well before the mass of beaming parents arrived. I went to her classroom and stopped outside the doorway, hoping she wouldn't see me. I was curious to see her interacting in a setting other than the familiarity of home life. What I saw next was uncharacteristic of what my wife and I had experienced. There she was, playing with a wooden kitchen play set similar to hers. Anytime other kids wanted to join in, she would quickly prevent them from touching her utensils. At one point, she snatched a spatula from another child's hand. This was the moment I decided to intervene, making my arrival known. I wouldn't say I dived across the room slowly to grab the spatula back from her. Like any good parent, I hunched down on my middle-aged knees and kindly asked her to play nice.

"Sweetie, let the other girl play with the spatula. It's the right thing to share and a space for everyone to play together."

She sulked and told me she wanted to make whatever she was making and that so-and-so wasn't welcome. At this point, I could feel all eyes on me and knew I couldn't leave her thinking what she did was right. I shifted to my life-lesson dad voice.

"Sweetie, you also need to allow others to play here. It's their space, too."

She sagged, arms hanging, head on her shoulder. I rubbed them up and down.

"You need to be nice and share things and allow others to make what they want to make even if you don't like it, okay?"

She let out a theatrical sigh. "Yessss dad-deee."

I watched as she stepped aside to allow the other boy to stir his pot of coloured pieces and make scrambled Lego.

Tolerance starts at a young age. Like children, we must endure playing together in the proverbial toy kitchen. We stand aside for those who want to potter beside us, expressing our way even if we think our way is best, and we are patient and waiting for our turn without quarrel and angst.

This chapter can get ahead of itself and wander off like a curious child in a supermarket. Yet, tolerance is necessary to consider the very theme of patience. It's also essential for it to stay bracketed. Tolerance once meant being indulgent, permissive, and lenient towards others' opinions and beliefs. Today, our culture has hijacked it, and it means something entirely different. The term characterises an attitude of forbearance in judging beliefs, behaviours, practices, and opinions in conflict with one's own. Patience used to have a different place than it did. It now sits on the proverbial bench, making a waterboy-like appearance, hydrating the red-faced and coarse throat of our irrational friend, intolerance. Forbearance can coexist with those whom you disagree with. It is possible but has yet to be practised.

The Parable of the Weeds beautifully illustrates this idea of tolerating others despite our differences. Just as my daughter needed to learn patience and tolerance when sharing her kitchen play set, the parable offers a similar lesson on living alongside others. The servants, eager to rid the field of weeds, ask the owner to remove them. But his response is surprising: "Let both grow together." In farming, this would seem absurd — yet it serves as a reminder that patience and tolerance are often necessary in life's complex and challenging moments. Much like we endure each other in everyday interactions, this parable teaches us to coexist with those who differ, waiting for judgment, like the harvest, will come. As Paul reminds us in Ephesians 4:2-3, Christians are called to "put up with one another in love" and to strive for unity through patience and humility. It's not an easy path, but as we face the daily challenges that test our tolerance, we're reminded of the deeper purpose behind enduring these moments with grace. Very rarely would you drift through the day without crossing paths with someone having a different temperament than your own.

Think about it. Your boss could be moody, your colleague churlish, your wife crabby, your friend unflattering, and your children belligerent. If you're unlucky, you could experience that all in one day. My mother always used to say, "When you bring two people together, two worlds are colliding at the same time." Impact doesn't always result in an explosion. Crossing paths, however, requires us to be mindful of our opposite world. The challenge is navigating different habits, peculiarities of taste, idiosyncrasies, dispositions, and convictions. My faith walk might differ from your journey, and yours might not even include God. The unpredictability and fallibility of human nature exacerbate life, especially when two worlds come together and focus on imperfections.

A friendship won't stand the test of time if the test goads trivial nitpicking and shortcomings. In marriage, 'nagging' has a similar effect. Say I were to nag my wife for every little misdemeanour; it would wear her down over time, and vice versa. In my previous book, I devoted an entire chapter to the expectations we place upon entering a romantic relationship. Anyone who expects their boyfriend, girlfriend, spouse, or husband to act or be a certain way is setting the relationship up to fail. The fruit of the Spirit bears no significance when exercising a spirit of fault-finding, rendering life anything but a blessing.

Instead, it is in our best interest to expect the unexpected. I don't mean it negatively. No one wants to treat every relationship like a Lucky Packet, hoping to find what you want. It's more about the mindset of discovery, the beauty in the journey, unboxing something new and beautiful, and allowing time to unfurl and flourish

---

Historically, Jesus warned his followers of the persecution to come. Some of the worst kinds of persecution followed in the years after Christ's ascension. It's no surprise when Paul addressed the church of Galatia, he emphasised tolerance. "There is neither Jew nor Greek, there is neither slave nor free, there is neither male nor female, for you are all one in Christ Jesus" (Galatians 3:28 NKJV). Rome's intolerance of unauthorised belief systems led to thousands, if not millions, of Christian deaths. The Diocletianic or Great Persecution was the last and most severe for Christians in 303 AD. It lasted eighteen months, and modern historians estimate that as many as three and a half thousand Christians were killed under the authority of the Imperial edicts. In a well-documented Roman letter (considered to be the first pagan account to refer Christianity) between Pliny the Younger to Emperor Trajan, he asks for guidance in dealing with Christians.[1]

---

1. From The Works of Josephus (tr. by William Whiston; Peabody: Hendrickson Publishers, 1987)

The stark reality is that neither Pliny nor the Emperor mentions any crimes committed. They faced a problem where the only wrongdoing was their belief contrary to Rome. After torturing two believers, Pliny concluded that Christianity was no more than a "squalid superstition".[2] The only crime was nonconformity—going against the populace. This meant abstaining from idolatry, which was rife in Rome. Ivor Davidson notes in his book on the Birth of the Church, "Roman society was thought to depend upon the the maintenance of *pax decorum*, the peace of the Gods".[3] Christianity threw everything into doubt, and Rome didn't want division stirred up in society. Rejecting idol worship was considered highly offensive, much like vandalising a statue or refusing to sing the national anthem today. Polarising social narratives like these have existed through the ages. Josh Moody, in a column for the Gospel Coalition, sums this up poignantly:

> "True tolerance depends on a contrary notion. Tolerance says, "I disagree with what you're saying, but I allow you the right to say it." But relativism says, "What you are arguing for is only relatively true, so you and I already agree." Relativism is intrinsically intolerant because it rejects right and wrong—and therefore any need for toleration.

---

2. (Ivor J.Davidson, The Birth of the Church, 197)
3. (Ivor J.Davidson, The Birth of the Church, 201)

> The Roman Empire had a version of relativistic tolerance. Only religions that worshiped the emperor and his gods were tolerated. That didn't play out too well for many—including the Christians who were tortured and killed for refusing to say, "Caesar is Lord." Medieval Christendom then exerted massive energy attempting to pick up the pieces after the Roman Empire fell. The church aligned closely with various military powers and leaders to protect the church and civilization. That strategy sullied the church through close association with military action."[4]

History indeed repeats itself, often for the wrong reasons. One only needs to reach for a school textbook to learn of a minority's demise at the hands of their oppressors. Whether discrimination of gender, race, or religion, humanity always wants to have a leg up. Pliny's correspondence shows that intolerance and impatience stem from fear and a lack of understanding. Instead of seeking to understand Christians and their faith, he defaults to fear — an irrational self-preservation of Roman rule and power against any opposing alternative. How different is the narrative today? The modern world faces similar opposing forces. Cancel culture or wokeness permeates social narratives within industry, politics, and religion. This new form

---

4. Josh Moody, The Gospel Coaltion, 'Does the Bible Promote Tolerance or Intolerance?', August 24, 2018, https://www.thegospelcoalition.org/article/bible-tolerance-intolerance/

of social justice attracts a mob-like mentality, persecuting their victims in the social arena, sometimes in twenty-three characters or less. This troll-like behaviour frightfully demands compliance, much like Roman society before Constantine. It's not just individuals behind screens but also peaceful (substitute car-burning) protesters, CRT-pushing university professors, and virtue-signalling corporations. They, by majority, disagree with any form of opposing, constructive criticism. In his book The Intolerance of Tolerance, Professor D.A. Carson points out a cultural move from an old intolerance to a new:

> "The shift from "accepting the existence of different views" to "acceptance of different views." From recognizing other people's right to have different beliefs or practices to accepting the differing views of other people, is subtle in form, but massive in substance. To accept that a different or opposing position exists and deserves the right to exist is one thing; to accept the position itself means that one is no longer opposing it. The new tolerance suggests that actually accepting another's position means believing that position to be true or at least as true as your own. We move from allowing the free expression of contrary opinion to the acceptance of all opinions; we leap from permitting the articulation of beliefs and claims with which we do not agree to asserting that all

beliefs and claims are equally valid. Thus we slide from the old tolerance to the new."[5]

In this "slide or shift", Carson talks about challenges the Christian view grounded in the absolutes of the Gospel. The cultural persuasion of accepting differences increasingly challenges Christians' faith and divine patience. This passivity unwillingly forces Christian opposition under the banner of intolerance or fundamentalism. Carson urges Christians to continue exposing secular neutrality as a threat to the Gospel of Christ but to do so with "practicing civility," which is "not to be confused with a weakening of Christian convictions." This doesn't mean our sole goal should be fighting against tolerance. Our mission is to win the world over with the good news of the Gospel, done with love and patience. Paul writes to Timothy, urging him to stick with the Gospel despite man's reluctance to hear it. "Preach the word; be prepared in season and out of season; correct, rebuke and encourage —with great patience and careful instruction" (2 Timothy 2 NKJV).

Inevitably, some will turn away from the truth, disheartened or defiant to the Gospel. They will seek pseudo-truths or follow what they believe is true to their selves. One only needs to doom-scroll through social media to get their truth algorithm. As we read in Timothy,

---

[5]. Carson, D. A.. The Intolerance of Tolerance. United States: Eerdmans Publishing Company, 2012. Pages 3-4

we must rebuke and encourage, always in love and patience and restored in such a spirit. Distorted truth happens when presenting biblical virtues as a natural position, but in most cases, they are personal preferences. This overlap can be deceptive and misleading, and as Christians, we need to be awake to the truth, not woke to it. The only way to see behind misleading social narratives is to discern why it's happening and turn to a biblical perspective. Trueman further points out,

> The problem with expressive individualism is not its emphasis on the dignity or the individual value of every human being...Rather, it is the fact that expressive individualism has detached these concepts of individual dignity and value from any kind of grounding in the sacred order...it [The West] had come to reject the created, divine image as the basis for its morality, and there was nothing left but a morass of competing tastes.[6]

As Christians, we're called to be in the world but not of it (John 15:19). The Bible warns us that the world will hate us for it. Following Christ means denying expressive individualism at its core. The world's ignorance reflects its hatred for the message of Christ. Many Christians hide behind this verse to avoid those who live by very different

---

6. Trueman, Carl R.. The Rise and Triumph of the Modern Self: Cultural Amnesia, Expressive Individualism, and the Road to Sexual Revolution. United States: Crossway, (n.d.). Pg 388

moral codes and belief systems. Theologian William Barclay wrote,

> We are sent out into the world to love one another. Sometimes we live as if we were sent into the world to compete with one another, or to dispute with one another, or even to quarrel with one another.[7]

Jesus' words are not a justification for avoidance or vindication for intolerance. His life demonstrates God's love for the world despite their hatred for Him. When He said, "...you are not of the world," He meant it both as a fact and an explanation. He reminds His disciples that they will receive hatred for their words, beliefs, and deeds, most of all for following a heretic, rabble-rouser, and madman. Christ continues to assure them to keep in mind that the world first hated Him, yet His love never waned. In the verse prior, Christ implores His disciples to bear fruit. Rooted in Christ means to bear the fruit of the Spirit, which means loving our neighbour as ourselves. Christ is handing them the tools to survive. It's like Bear Grylls sharing knowledge before you drop from a chopper into a jungle of darkness. Christ encourages all to go deep into the world, but we must follow His teachings to survive. "If you remain in me and I in you, you will bear much fruit..." if you remain in my love, you will keep in my commands"

---

7. Barclay, William, 1907-1978. Growing in Christian Faith: A book of daily readings, Westminster John Knox Press, pg 13

(John 15:5-10 NIV). We will still love, still be kind, and still be patient. Jesus also precedes "bear fruit" with "Go," commanding them to live this out in the world actively. To not hide, avoid, or seclude ourselves is not a passive word where we live in our Sunday bubble. We don't need to live like Ned Flanders. He would still love his 'unsavoury' neighbours in the enigmatic town of Springfield.

"Dear Neighbour, you are my brother. I love you, and yet I feel a great sadness in my bosom."[8]

No doubt tolerance is a vast subject to cover in just one chapter. I've only skimmed the surface. I hope that the message resonates with Christians. Albert Barnes' commentary on Ephesians 4:2 beautifully captures the essence of walking according to the will of God —walking as Christ walked:

> It is in such gentle and quiet virtues as meekness and forbearance, that the happiness and usefulness of life consist, far more than in brilliant eloquence, in splendid talent, or illustrious deeds, that shall send the name to future times. It is the bubbling spring which flows gently; the little rivulet which glides through the meadow, and which runs along day and night by the farmhouse, that is useful, rather than the swollen flood or the roaring

---

8. Ned Flanders, 'The Simpsons', Season Two, Episode Six

cataract. Niagara excites our wonder; and we stand amazed at the power and greatness of God there, as he "pours it from his hollow hand." But one Niagara is enough for a continent or a world; while that same world needs thousands and tens of thousands of silver fountains, and gently flowing rivulets, that shall water every farm, and every meadow, and every garden, and that shall flow on, every day and every night, with their gentle and quiet beauty. So with the acts of our lives. It is not by great deeds only, like those of Howard - not by great sufferings only, like those of the martyrs - that good is to be done; it is by the daily and quiet virtues of life - the Christian temper, the meek forbearance, the spirit of forgiveness in the husband, the wife, the father, the mother, the brother, the sister, the friend, the neighbor - that good is to be done; and in this all may be useful.[9]

When applied correctly, the biblical narrative is rich and conclusive on human dignity across the categorical scripture. There is no watered-down, sub-standard alternate version. This very narrative calls us to sow seeds, not root out weeds. May you all show spiritual concern for your brothers and sisters. Do so through love and patience, not through verbal harvesting.

---

9. https://biblehub.com/commentaries/barnes/ephesians/4.htm.

A God Given Restraint

Our patience is a proof of our faith in God's timing and love.

— Oswald Chambers

It was a typical cold, dull winter morning in late March. My friend Marty and I decided to meet and head out to Glendalough Lake, a steady hour's drive southwest of Dublin. I had been living in Ireland for the past year and was itching to dust off my fly-fishing box of dry and wet lures. The last time I caught a rainbow trout was when my parents and I had taken a trip around the South Island of New Zealand. As much as I was keen to snag one or two, I couldn't wait to head out to such a beautiful and historical part of Wicklow County. Glendalough, meaning

Valley of the Two Lakes, epitomises the rugged, romantic Irish landscape. Substantial remains of an ancient monastic settlement pepper the surroundings. The clipped, bell-like, head-girlish voice of the car's satnav prompted the last left turn to our destination. In the distance, I saw the dark, mysterious lake tucked into a long, glacial valley fringed by forest. As we approached, it felt profoundly tranquil and somewhat mystical. Catching a glimpse of the looming thousand-year-old Round Tower, it made sense why the solitude-seeking monks settled here.

"Do you know why these monks built such high towers?" Marty asked.

"Haven't a clue," I replied.

"Well, look up there on the left. Can you see it?"

"The one that looks like a doorway a couple of meters up?"

"Yeah, that's it. What's it doing up there?" I asked.

"Well, they would pull the ladder up and take refuge in the towers when Vikings and such attacked their monastery."

"Smart," I mumbled.

Upon our ascent, we reached the bank of the lake and admired the view. It was teardrop-silver in colour and womb-quiet. Avenues of pine trees standing to attention flanked the surrounding edges. The peppery scent of mint percolated towards us. We cast our lines across the glorious lustre of water as our flies lightly dapped across without affecting the mountain's reflection. I feasted my eyes on the poetic vignette and waited. Unlike Marty, I was less concerned about the angling particulars and ceremonial pleasures. While he stood leg-deep in waders and ironic outdoor flannel, I was getting antsy for a catch. The thing about fly-fishing, or any fishing for that matter, is the anticipation of the catch. Of course, it's about the immediate and tactile and being in the angler's zone. To maintain that zone requires the environment to lead you and the experience you're in. It's not about bringing your world and all its conditions into it. There has to be an element of surrender, without getting esoteric, to nature. This is particularly great in theory but altogether contrary in practice. In my case, I was seeing Marty out of the corner of my eye reeling in trout, after flaming trout boiled my blood. With zero bites on my slack line, I whipped my rod back in frustration and gave an aggravated yelp. It echoed in the hollowness of the valley. The lake lost its Feng-shui shine and became the devil's broth as far as I was concerned.

"You're scaring the fish away!" Marty echoed.

"I've been moving up and down, and the fish are giving me nothing!" I yelled.

Moments later, we reeled in our lines along with the setting sun. Marty sidled up and put his arm around my shoulder. He squeezed me tightly as if to inject what he was saying deep into my bones.

"Mate, no one catches a fish in anger."

He was right. Anger never attracts anything. It's not a beacon; it's a warning sign triggered when we can't control physical or emotional pain. The happy medium, of course, is patience. As I looked out on the lake, I felt frustrated with my lack of accomplishment. Ergo, there is a need for more patience. Frustration from needing to know where a problem lies is a sign of impatience. Losing my calm over rainbow trout could be the result of many things. How I cast, what lures I use, where I drop my line, where the fish might gather, and so on. It comes down to wisdom, but even intelligent people can do stupid things. I could have the art of fly-fishing down to a tee, but there will always be unknowns. The fish might not be hungry. Something might have spooked them. There might be a disturbance in the water. Rain could have caused chemicals and clay to leave the water murky white, muddy brown, or yellow. Wisdom transcends mere readiness; it is the profound gift of discerning the vast, intricate panorama of existence.

A friend once told me, "Anger is hard to deal with; patience is hard to develop." I, for one, can testify to that. When my father passed away, it was like I inherited a spirit of anger. My father wasn't an angry man, nor was his father before him. They would lose their patience at the slightest thing. My father would get annoyed if he heard the faintest sound of a dog barking blocks away. When you're angry, the more you lose your patience, the angrier you become. Trivial things start to annoy you. I noticed this starting to play out in my own life. Often, I would direct my annoyance toward our family dog, Zulu. He isn't warrior-like in temperament, but his breed's designed to flush out the enemy. In his case, anything that moved. Most notably, this 'gundog' breed lives a high-octane life, and the passive has no place for him and his kind. Eager to please is an understatement. Hyperactive and incredibly needy is more like it. While I love him, his attention-craving would wear thin on me. To make matters worse, he shed more hair than a St. Petersburg socialite in a mink coat. Such crimes forced me to relegate him from the house to the backyard. It was all trivial at the surface level in the greater scheme of things. Anger isn't the why; it's the how. As the authors of the book The Boy Crisis describe, "Anger is our vulnerabilities mask."[1] My anger was attributed to my impatience in dismissing much deeper-rooted problems. It's an avoidance mechanism — removing ourselves from any opportunity that brings pain or hurt. As Dr. David J. Lieberman points out, "Pain in and of itself does not lead to anger," but it's that which we cannot control. My frustration at not catching fish or my dog's malting might have nothing to do with the situation. It might be a manifestation learned in all areas of life. In other words, losing my patience in one situation becomes a habit for all situations. We see this lack of control in our minds as a weakness — a reflection of our capabilities as human beings. I may not be in control, but I will show whoever's in my way who's boss. All one needs to do is look closely at the word impatience and discover the first two letters pointing back to you. I'm in control. I'm going to handle this. I'm not going to wait any longer. I'm going

---

1. Gray, John., Farrell, Warren. The Boy Crisis: Why Our Boys Are Struggling and What We Can Do About It. United States: BenBella Books, 2018. Chapter 20

to react now. I'm annoyed. What you're saying behind the facade of control is, "I'm selfish." And that, my friend, is what leads to impatience. This sense of always needing to take control is ego. Lieberman points out, "human beings experience two primary emotions: love (which is soul-based) and fear (which is ego-based). All positive emotions stem from love, and all negative emotions stem from fear...".[2] As we have learned, love is patience (which I'll address in the next chapter). Fear comes back to feeling isolated and not in control. Again, it's about controlling the uncontrollable. As much as our ego leads us to believe we cannot control everything in life. We can, however, learn to control the way we react. It is possible to put our emotions into practice. If we allow our feelings to dictate every response, we leave very little room for intellect to lead. That doesn't mean we need to be void of feelings but allow one to come before the other. If I get angry about a salesperson phoning me and interrupting my dinner, my emotions shape my reaction. But if I were to step back and assume this might be a family man missing dinner with his family so he can put food on the table, then my intellect leads. Logic inevitably defeats anger. People who do not allow their own ego to lead open themselves up to humility and compassion for others. Anger can only exist when 'I'm' jumps ahead of patience.

---

2. Lieberman, Dr. David J.. Never Get Angry Again: The Foolproof Way to Stay Calm and in Control in Any Conversation Or Situation. United States: St. Martin's Publishing Group, 2018.

Patience diffuses anger. Or let me put it this way: patience diffuses reacting out of anger. When Paul says love is 'slow to anger' and 'is not easily angered,' he's not inferring love eradicates anger. He's using the adverbs "slow to" and "not easily" to describe the gradual dissemination. Loving the way Paul calls us to is not flipping the lid and seeing red. In both instances of anger, the Greek refers to it as 'slowly proving' or the 'coming wrath.' In other words, it's permitting to practice patience as the anger is not immediate. We find similarities in this approach throughout the Old Testament.

God had many opportunities to lash out against the people He tried to save who rejected His promises. Countless times, God patiently called Israel out on their sins and to change their ways. God doesn't renege on His promises, but He certainly is just (Isaiah 5:25). Israel's rebellious ways ultimately led them into exile in Babylon. Before I go any further, I have a good idea of what most of you are thinking. Let's take a slight detour and allow me to address the proverbial elephant in the room. If we're talking about love and patience, why does a loving and patient God get angry? This is a profoundly theological question, one which takes considered thought. I'll give a quick snapshot for the sake of moving on. Firstly, God's anger is very different from the emotional anger we experience as humans. We cannot simply apply our human experience of anger to God and expect it to be the same as divine anger. It's what theologians call anthropomorphic. However, we can learn from how God responds to things.

Secondly, God's anger isn't sporadic, undeserved, unmeasured, or irrational. It's always underpinned by love. The theologian John Stott alludes to this,

> "For there is nothing capricious or arbitrary about the holy God. Nor is he ever irascible, malicious, spiteful or vindictive. His anger is neither mysterious nor irrational. It is never unpredictable but always predictable, because it is provoked by evil and by evil alone."[3]

God is love. We shouldn't think of God as angry and loving. Love is an attribute of God, and His wrath is a response to sin. Equally, Paul never refers to God's anger as an attitude towards man. It's more that his anger was a result of the consequences of sin.[4] Many theologians believe this is the cause and effect of a moral universe. When God is angry, it's always because people turn away towards images that man has created themselves. If we are made in the image of God and worship something else, wouldn't that be a smack in the face of God? God calls this idolatry. Again, do you see the common denominator? The word begins with an emphatic I. I want money, I want power, I want sex. I like [...] We aggrandise ourselves and place our image above all else. Idolatry begets idolatry. We no longer see God in us. Some Christian leaders have

---

3. Stott, John. The Cross of Christ. United Kingdom: InterVarsity Press, 2012. PG 171
4. C. H. Dodd, *The Epistle of Paul to the Romans*, 2nd ed. (London and Glasgow: Collins, 1959), pp. 47-50.

professed in sermons we are mini-Gods because we're in His image. Let's get something clear here: there is only one God. We are made in His image and are not created to be Gods of any shape, size, or kind. Yet, we have the nerve to question why God shows anger in the Bible. So we come back to anger.

Upon reading the central message of the Old and New Testament, we learn patience is a "God-given" restraint. This type of patience is best operated when faced with opposing forces. This is evident when the Jews mocked and taunted Christ for His unwavering declaration as the Son of God. Imagine, for a second, a traffic cop pulling you over in a roadblock. A burly officer saunters over, knocks on your window, and asks you to show your driver's license. You do so obligingly, only for the officer to proceed to chastise you. He questions the validity of your name and date of birth on your official license.

Now, you could either argue and become aggressive and face a hefty fine or worse, or you could dig deep and be Christ-like. Patience takes practice; in many senses, it's a hard-fought everyday struggle. In this sense, patience is the solution to the proverbial Gordian knot life often throws at you. Patience will never come easy; it's something we have to fight for every day. In Ephesians 6:11, Paul talks about putting on the spiritual armour of God. Although we can't physically wear it, we can draw confidence in trusting in Him to give us the strength to endure.

By doing so, we can act in a way that is true to our faith in that promise. We can firmly plant our feet on a promise that patience is a discipline God gives. Not something cooked up entirely from our strength. It doesn't mean we're absolved from practising patience; we can also seek it from Him in hardships. We might not curb our anger immediately. However, we will start to notice that the power of our anger is weakening, short-lived, and not bent into hate. Ultimately, if anger is the mind that wishes the worst upon others, patience is the mind that holds it back. Patience transcends from love and is something we live out because we are called to love God with all our minds (Matthew 22:37). From this (first) commandment, the second will flow from our actions toward our neighbours.

Patience and Love: An Unlikely Partnership

> The lovers of God never run out of patience, for they know that time is needed for the crescent moon to become full.
>
> — Shams Tabrizi

MANY YEARS AGO, WHILE PLANNING MY WEDDING with my wife, there were two non-negotiables. First, Canon D Major by Pachelbel was out of the question. The sluggishly slow ascent indicated the perfect cadence for a bridal procession. To my wife, it was a bridal metronome of sonic torture. To recall her words, "It's an overused sappy composition. I'd rather walk down the aisle to the sound of nails scratching a chalkboard." Years later, Ed Sheeran covered it. Now, thousands of brides march and swoon to his chart-topping rendition. In hindsight, I have to agree with my wife. The second no-no was the famous, biblical "Love Chapter" — 1 Corinthians 13:4-8. If I recall correctly, the latter was my sway, but we were unanimous.

Although a wedding favourite, it has become, in my mind, a wedding cliché that has lost its meaning. Even so, there are still lessons to be learned. Let's look closer at the first sentence. "Love is patient" makes sense in hindsight. It's like a fine wine; give it a couple of years to marinate, and then you'll taste its robust and complex flavours. Paul is speaking of something quite profound. He's pointing to a patience (makrothymei) that is long-suffering and enduring. It's not immediate; it's passive. As you read the second part of the sentence, you'll see that it's active, suggesting a charitable display of love. The King James infers, "Charity suffereth long and is kind." Although opposite in definition, they are both part of the same sentence. It takes patience (long-suffering) to accept someone else's actions that might test you. Acknowledging doing good for others requires kindness (charity, full service). Simply put, love endures evils and bestows blessings.

The apostle is attributing love to a person, but equally, this is the divine grace of God with His people. In essence, it's the application of the first two commandments. The love of God, and for our neighbour for His good, is patient to ALL men. Furthermore, it's a reference to the spiritual gifts. It's no coincidence that the chapter before this one is all about spiritual gifts. One should read it as a whole — the what followed by the how. His conjunction begins

Patience and Love: An Unlikely Partnership 171

with the last statement leading into the next chapter, "But now let me show you a way of life that is best of all" (1 Cor. 12:31 NET). All Christians need to practice these gifts, but they are meaningless without a love that binds them together. These gifts are given by the grace of God's divine love. Neither faith nor hope can warrant the existence of these gifts; only love can. In light of this, it makes sense that patience is a spiritual gift possible only through God's divine love, manifested in His faithful servants. While anyone can practice patience, love does not always motivate it. As Paul insists, everything else is meaningless without love. When describing God, Peter implies a patient love, "The Lord is not slow concerning his promise, as some regard slowness, but is being patient toward you, because he does not wish for any to perish but for all to come to repentance" (2 Peter 3:9 NET). Like a stubborn teenager finally unlocking their bedroom door and making their way to dinner, the Bible is filled with stories of people not listening to God but eventually coming around. God's patience comes from everlasting love and long-suffering for your sake. It endures despite it feeling like a delay at times.

Every other gift might wane and waver, but love exists forever. What's even more interesting is that Paul isn't writing to Corinth about emotional love; it's not about what love is. He highlights the verb and describes the actions he's challenging the Corinthian church to put into practice. His description of patience is a call to the church to be active, persist, and pursue it, which is why I disdain its wedding recital. I wouldn't object if everyone understood the grace of God's divine, everlasting love and Paul's purposeful intention towards us as a church. It's the answer to the question, how must a wife stand by her husband when he's in a coma? Or how must a husband carry the weight of a family while his wife's depression ravages him? In faith and hope, the actual test of what Paul is talking about is choosing patient love in an everlasting way, regardless of future circumstances. A love like this isn't self-serving but outward-oriented so that spiritual gifts can flourish — not by our strength, but through Christ.

In a chapter in my previous book, I discuss love being a choice—the antithesis of feeling. It's not something a lovestruck teenager does. We repeatedly pour over a love letter, relishing every inked word (who writes letters anymore?). Ultimately, love becomes a decision no matter how many emojis or handwritten notes lift the heart. To quote my own words, "Love can be effortless and equally an effort." The wings of a butterfly can carry love for only so long. We all know how short-lived their life cycle is. There will come a time when true love rises despite trying circumstances. It's how we respond that counts. Paul's active and passive love verbs express a foundation of longsuffering and benevolence. He doesn't say love is like; it simply is. We do not differentiate between attraction, affection, and affinity in reading love. Instead, we broadly apply it like thick, long strokes of peanut butter across a slice of bread. Modern-day terms like "I love grilled cheese sandwiches," "I love my mom," and "I love lazy days in the sun." We do not distinguish love the way the Greeks did and not the way Paul intended in Corinthians. As Christians, we should never relegate love solely to something we must do. We should keep love as feeling-filled as possible. The scriptures certainly do not instruct us to love our neighbours and enemies through action alone. Accordingly, agapao (to love) renders the action of living through and in Christ (1 John 4:16). Paul suggests living a "spirit-filled life," thereby espousing God's will. In this sense, God defines it as an act of appropriating affection involving choice and selection, not out of stubbornness or obligation. As part of our faith, there must be a heart element and affection that prompts and enjoins. It matters not whether the love expresses itself in scripture or the soul.

The Bible has four unique forms of love, each with its use and meaning: Eros, storge, philia, and agape — romantic, familial, brotherly, and divine love. The love Paul is referring to in Corinthians is agape. In the New Testament, it typically refers to divine love, but mostly what we would understand as benevolence or selfless love. In other words, a love that doesn't need any gain in return. It's given love, which the Greeks also refer to in its plural form as "love feasts." That word conjures a banquet of delicious food, wine, and good conversation, maybe even jazz on vinyl for the hipsters. As we practice today, such feasts seemed to exist among Christians before the Lord's Supper and communion. The thing about this love is it's the highest form of the four loves, demanding the utmost of us. It's not a love by default or by blood. In context to the verse, the attributes that follow this love, patience, kindness, and so on, require work and effort from us. The giddy love of romance will not hold tight when someone slights you. Agape love endures and selflessly gives.

Though Paul does not describe marriage as an institution, his description of love within the construct of marriage inadvertently perfectly illustrates God's love. There are trials and tribulations in every marriage. When we are unfaithful, unloving, unrepentant, unforgiving, unhappy, unapproachable, ungracious, uncontrollable, unapologetic, unemotional, unchanging, and unimpassioned, God remains ever faithful, ever patient, and ever loving, a love that is steadfast and long-suffering. Paul's words are radical but not unthinkable. At times, this standard might seem unattainable, but it is the standard he calls the church to uphold. It's how we should show patience and kindness towards one another grounded in love. Marriage is the ultimate display of this — a covenant, a pre-eminent symbol of God's covenant with the chosen people of Israel. All traditional wedding vows reflect God's patience and kindness, with slight variations across denominations. Jewish wedding vows, in particular, are closest to this. The groom places the ring on the bride's finger and says, "Haray at mekudeshet lee beh-taba'at zo keh-dat Moshe veh-Yisrael," which translated reads, "Behold, with this ring you are consecrated to me according to the laws of Moses and Israel." In the Jewish faith, this moment of betrothal is called Kiddushin in Hebrew, meaning sanctification. It is to be set apart and made holy — a vessel or house where God dwells. It's no coincidence that Paul opens the chapter in verse two by writing, "To the church of God in Corinth, to those sanctified in Christ Jesus and called to be holy, together with all those everywhere who call on the name of our Lord Jesus Christ, their Lord and ours..." (1 Cor. 1:2 NIV).

'Patient love' occurs when the Holy Spirit dwells within us and commits us as a church and body of Christ to loving God, loving our neighbours, and loving each other 'patiently'. This kind of patient love surfaces unity, purpose, and strength. The 'agape' love we adopt suggests that we see the world through new eyes, seeing a picture that transcends our petty worlds and realities. It isn't self-serving or short-sighted but on God's timing with eternal relevance. We are seeing and working towards a common purpose, a bigger picture — a kingdom perspective. When we do this, we finally understand what Paul means in Greek when we translate the verse verbatim into English, 'love patients'. He is illustrating what God does and how he behaves and, inevitably, for us as Christians to see all people through the eyes of Christ.

. . .

This brings us full circle to understanding that love, in its most accurate form, is not just a feeling but a conscious act of will. It is the choice to be patient, endure, and act kindly even when circumstances do not favour it. Just as the lovers of God never run out of patience, for they know that time is needed for the crescent moon to become whole, we, too, must learn to be patient, allowing our love to grow and mature. In doing so, we reflect the divine love that is patient, kind, and eternal, binding us together in the unity of Christ's love. This is the essence of the lesson Paul imparts to the Corinthians and, by extension, to us all.

Conclusion

Patience, at its core, is more than just waiting. It's a deep exercise in faith, endurance, and wisdom. Through the stories we've explored, from biblical accounts to personal experiences, we see that patience is an active, dynamic force shaping our character and perspective.

Patience balances accepting what is and engaging with what could be. It's about enduring discomfort and uncertainty gracefully while moving purposefully toward our goals. This virtue is essential for navigating the complexities and unpredictabilities of life. When we face challenges, whether minor daily hassles or significant life events, patience gives us the strength to keep going and the insight to reflect on our learning.

Patience is a countercultural virtue in a world that prizes speed and instant gratification. It teaches us to slow down, appreciate the journey, and trust life's timing. Patience isn't just about waiting for things to happen and maintaining hope and perseverance in tough times. It's about recognising that real growth often occurs during these periods of waiting.

Patience is closely linked with humility, self-control, and compassion. It requires us to be present in the moment, appreciating the process rather than fixating on the end goal. As we develop patience, we gain a deeper appreciation for life's complexities and the lessons it brings.

Patience reflects God's character. The Bible often highlights God's patience, not wanting anyone to perish but everyone to come to repentance (2 Peter 3:9). This divine patience shows His boundless love and mercy, setting an example for us to follow. As Christians, we're called to mirror this patience in our interactions with others and in our relationship with God.

In our spiritual journey, patience is an act of faith. It signifies our trust in God's perfect timing and plan for our lives. It challenges us to let go of our anxieties and impatience, knowing that God's ways are higher than our ways and His thoughts are higher than our thoughts (Isaiah 55:9). By cultivating patience, we align ourselves with God's will, allowing His Spirit to work within us, producing the fruit of patience that glorifies Him.

Ultimately, patience is a testament to our endurance capacity and faith in God's unfolding plan. It reminds us that even in the most challenging times, there is value in waiting, trusting the process, and believing that our efforts and sacrifices will yield meaningful results. By embracing patience, we open ourselves to growth, wisdom, and a deeper understanding of God's purpose for us.

So, let's not see patience as a burden but as a powerful force that enriches our lives and deepens our relationship with God. Let it guide us through our struggles, shape our character, and inspire us to live with grace and resilience. May patience be our steadfast companion as we continue our journeys, helping us navigate life's complexities with hope and unwavering faith. Embrace patience as the chrysalis of our transformation, essential for the emergence of our true, fully realised selves in Christ. And let's always remember that our patience reflects the divine patience God extends to us daily, a testament to His enduring love and faithfulness.

Acknowledgments

Writing this book has been a journey of reflection, discovery, and immense growth. As I complete this project, I am deeply grateful to the many individuals who have supported and inspired me.

First and foremost, I owe a debt of gratitude to my wife, whose unwavering patience and encouragement have been my anchor. Your love and support have made this journey possible, and I dedicate this book to you.

To my daughters, Ferne and Ivy, thank you for being my constant source of joy and teaching me the true meaning of patience. Your curious minds and boundless energy remind me daily of the beauty of the present moment.

I want to thank my editor, Roy Cooper, whose keen insights and meticulous attention to detail have significantly improved this manuscript. Your dedication and expertise have been invaluable, and I sincerely appreciate your hard work.

Thanks to my agent, Gwen Arnold, for believing in this project and guiding me through the publishing process with wisdom and grace.

To my friends and family, your words of encouragement and understanding have kept me motivated. Thank you for your patience and for giving me the time and space to write.

I am also grateful to the numerous scholars, authors, and thinkers whose works have informed and inspired the content of this book. Your contributions to theology, philosophy, and psychology have shaped my understanding of patience.

Finally, to my readers, thank you for embarking on this journey with me. I hope this book offers you new insights and perspectives on the virtue of patience and inspires you to embrace the beauty of waiting well.

With gratitude,
Stephen

July 2024

Scriptural Index

1 Corinthians 13:4	Page 183
1 Corinthians 13:7	Page 67
1 Corinthians 13:7	Page 197
1 Corinthians 13:14	Page 197
1 Corinthians 4:10	Page 140
1 Corinthians 4:10	Page 197
1 John 4:16	Page 186
1 John 4:17	Page 197
1 John 4:17	Page 149
1 Kings 11:1	Page 197, 120
1 Kings 4:29	Page 119, 197
1 Peter 1:13	Page 37, 197
1 Peter 3:20	Page 134, 197
1 Thessalonians 1:2	Page 197
1 Thessalonians 5:14	Page 88, 128, 197
1 Timothy 1:16	Page 136, 197
1 Timothy 2:3	Page 144, 197
2 Corinthians 3:17	Page 89, 197
2 Corinthians 6:4	Page 125, 127, 197
2 Peter 3:8	Page 25, 197
2 Peter 3:9	Page 184, 192, 197
2 Thessalonians 1:4	Page 125, 197
Acts 1:4	Page 47, 197
Acts 7:10	Page 119, 197
Acts 7:20	Page 119, 197
Colossians 1:11	Page 125, 197
Colossians 3:2	Page 88, 197
Corinthians 13:14	Page 33, 128
Daniel 5:11	Page 119, 197
Deuteronomy 34:9	Page 197
Ecclesiastes 7:8	Page 35, 88, 197

Scriptural Index

Ephesians 4:2	Page 129, 170, 197, 161
Ephesians 6:11	Page 180, 197
Exodus 31:18	Page 27, 198
Exodus 34:6	Page 134, 143, 198
Ezekiel 18:23	Page 144, 198
Galatians 3:28	Page 163, 198
Galatians 5:16	Page 153, 154, 151, 156, 198
Galatians 5:22	Page 87, 148, 198
Galatians 6:9	Page 128, 198
Genesis 15:1	Page 198
Genesis 1:1	Page 21, 198
Genesis 21:5	Page 126, 198
Genesis 22:17	Page 134, 198
Genesis 25:21	Page 126, 198
Genesis 29:18	Page 127, 198
Genesis 3:15	Page 134, 198
Genesis 6:3	Page 134
Hebrews 11:23	Page 141, 198
Hebrews 5:9	Page 97, 198
Hebrews 6:11	Page 67, 198
Isaiah 5:25	Page 152, 155, 178, 198
Isaiah 46:10	Page 138, 198
Isaiah 55:9	Page 198
Isaiah 64:8	Page 128, 198
James 1:2	Page 125, 157, 198
James 5:7	Page 136, 198
James 5:10	Page 135, 198
James 5:11	Page 198
John 6:35	Page 56, 198
John 15:7	Page 56, 198
John 15:5	Page 170, 198
John 15:8	Page 198
John 15:9	Page 56, 198
John 15:19	Page 168, 198
Joshua 14:10	Page 127, 198
Luke 21:29	Page 118

Scriptural Index   185

Luke 8:11 .... Page 152, 155, 199
Matt 24:32 .... Page 118
Matthew 11:28 .... Page 27, 199
Matthew 16:24 .... Page 84, 199
Matthew 22:37 .... Page 181, 199
Matthew 25:14 .... Page 67, 199
Nehemiah 9:17 .... Page 135, 199
Nehemiah 9:30 .... Page 33, 199
Numbers 12:3 .... Page 134, 199
Philippians 3:7 .... Page 78, 199
Philippians 4:8 .... Page 37, 199
Proverbs 17:27 .... Page 120
Psalm 149:7 .... Page 65, 199
Psalm 62:12 .... Page 199, 202, 124
Romans 12:12 .... Page 129, 199
Romans 15:4 .... Page 125, 199
Romans 15:5 .... Page 129, 199
Romans 2:4 .... Page 142, 199
Romans 2:6 .... Page 124, 199
Romans 5:3 .... Page 125, 127, 199
Romans 8:25 .... Page 125, 199
Romans 9:22 .... Page 135, 143, 199
Thessalonians 1:2 .... Page 67, 73, 47

Glossary

Introduction
1. Stephen Hawking, A Brief History of Time (New York: Bantam, 1998), 49.

The Genesis of Patience
2. Helge Kragh, Big Bang: the etymology of a name, Astronomy & Geophysics, Volume 54, Issue 2, April 2013, Pages 2.28–2.30, https://doi.org/10.1093/astrogeo/atto35
3. Siegel, E, 2019, Forbes Magazine, What Came First: Inflation Or The Big Bang?
4. Does God Exist? William Lane Craig vs. Christopher Hitchens. Biola University, La Mirada, California - April 4, 2009. https://www.youtube.com/watch?v=otYm41hb48o
5. Does God Exist? The Craig-Hitchens Debate. William Lane Craig vs. Christopher Hitchens. Biola University, La Mirada, California - April 4, 2009. https://www.reasonablefaith.org/media/debates/does-god-exist

Virtues of Patience
1. Economou, George., Langland, William. William Langland's "Piers Plowman": The C Version. United States: University of Pennsylvania Press, Incorporated, 1996, 209.
2. https://en.wikipedia.org/wiki/Transposed_letter_effect#Internet_meme
3. Spiegel, James S. How to Be Good in a World Gone Bad: Living a Life of Christian Virtue. United States: Kregel Publications, 2004.

Active versus Passive
1. "Keep calm and carry on." — British Government, 1939 motivational poster.
2. STULBERG, BRAD, SEPTEMBER 8, The Secret to Success?

Mastering the Art of Patience. TIME MAGAZINE 2021, https://time.com/6095843/learning-patience/

Waiting Well
1. Mischel W, Ebbesen EB, Zeiss AR. Cognitive and attentional mechanisms in delay of gratification. J Pers Soc Psychol. 1972 Feb;21(2):204-18. doi: 10.1037/h0032198. PMID: 5010404.
2. Bandak, Andreas, and Mette K. Janeja. "Introduction: Worth the Wait." In The Power of Waiting: Doubt, Hope, and Uncertainty, 1-18. OAPEN Library, 2018.
3. Gladwell, Malcolm. Outliers: The Story of Success. United Kingdom: Penguin Books Limited, 2008.
4. STULBERG, BRAD, SEPTEMBER 8, The Secret to Success? Mastering the Art of Patience. TIME MAGAZINE 2021, https://time.com/6095843/learning-patience/

Endurance and Perseverance in Practice
1. https://www.independent.co.uk/arts-entertainment/art/features/david-blaine-london-glass-box-stunt-reaction-starvation-above-the-below-a8523606.html
2. https://www.merriam-webster.com/dictionary/ultra

Losing your Patience
1. Nouwen, Henri J. M.. Bread for the Journey: A Daybook of Wisdom and Faith. United States: HarperCollins, 2009, page 5.
2. Leo Tolstoy, War and Peace, Book Ten, 1812.

The Practice of Patience
1. Wallace, David Foster. Infinite Jest. Little, Brown and Company, 1996.
2. Best English Speeches: David Foster Wallace "This is Water." (with BIG Subtitles).

The Beauty in Stillness
1. Smith, Jeffrey K., and Lisa F. Smith. "Spending Time on Art." Empirical Studies of the Arts 19, no. 2 (July 2001): 229–36.

2. Roberts, Jennifer L. The Power of Patience: Teaching students the value of deceleration and immersive attention. November 2013. www.harvardmagazine.com/sites/default/files/pdf/2013/11-pdfs/1113-40.pdf

How to Peel an Orange

1. Plato. The Republic. Translated by G.M.A. Grube, revised by C.D.C. Reeve. Indianapolis: Hackett Publishing Company, 1992, 514a-520a.
2. à Kempis, Thomas. The Imitation of Christ. Translated by William Creasy. Notre Dame, IN: Ave Maria Press, 1989, 39.
3. Schnitker, S. A., & Emmons, R. A. (2007). Patience as a virtue: Religious and psychological perspectives. Research in the Social Scientific Study of Religion, 18, 177–207.

Wisdom in Waiting

1. Nelson Mandela (2012). "Notes to the Future: Words of Wisdom", p.37, Simon and Schuster Venter, Sahm., Hatang, S. K.., Abrams, Douglas B.., Mandela, Nelson. Notes to the Future: Words of Wisdom. United States: Atria Books, 2012.
2. This interview appeared in the April 2001 issue of O, The Oprah Magazine. Read more.
3. Discourses I, 15.7–8 (Epictetus).

The Formation of Character

1. Psalm 62:12; Prov. 24:12.
2. Strong, James. "G5281 - hupomonē - Strong's Greek Lexicon (KJV).

Waiting for God

1. Nouwen, Henri J. M.. Here and Now: Living in the Spirit. United Kingdom: Crossroad Publishing Company, 2001, pg 31.
2. Notes on the Bible, by Albert Barnes, [1834], at 3 and 4.
3. Hocking, D. "The Patience of God by David Hocking." Blue Letter Bible. Last Modified 11 Aug, 2010.

The Fourth Fruit

1. McClymond, Michael James., McClymond, Michael J., McDermott, Gerald R., The Theology of Jonathan Edwards. United Kingdom: Oxford University Press, USA, 2012.
2. Keller, Timothy. Galatians for You. United Kingdom: Good Book Company, 2013.

Tolerance and Patience
1. From The Works of Josephus (tr. by William Whiston; Peabody: Hendrickson Publishers, 1987).
2. (Ivor J.Davidson, , 197).
3. (Ivor J.Davidson, , 201).
4. à Kempis, Thomas. The Imitation of Christ. Translated by William Creasy. Notre Dame, IN: Ave Maria Press, 1989, 39.
5. Carson, D. A.. The Intolerance of Tolerance. United States: Eerdmans Publishing Company, 2012. Pages 3-4.

God Given Restraint
1. Gray, John., Farrell, Warren. The Boy Crisis: Why Our Boys Are Struggling and What We Can Do About It. United States: BenBella Books, 2018. Chapter 20.
2. Lieberman, Dr. David J., Never Get Angry Again: The Foolproof Way to Stay Calm and in Control in Any Conversation Or Situation. United States: St. Martin's Publishing Group, 2018.
3. Stott, John. The Cross of Christ. United Kingdom: InterVarsity Press, 2012. PG 171.
4. A version of this article appears in print on March 1, 2012, Section A, Page 1 of the New York edition with the headline: For Impatient Web Users, an Eye Blink Is Just Too Long to Wait.

About the Author

Stephen Peter Anderson is an emerging author of political biographies. This is Stephen's third book.

Also by Stephen Peter Anderson

Wanderlust: How I Learned Rethink Love and Unlearn Lust

WANDERLUST

HOW I LEARNED TO RETHINK LOVE AND UNLEARN LUST

STEPHEN PETER ANDERSON

www.ingramcontent.com/pod-product-compliance
Lightning Source LLC
Chambersburg PA
CBHW022056290426
44109CB00014B/1118